CLIENT TESTIMONIALS ABOUT MICHELLE L. STEFFES

"I took Michelle's coach program. Everyone should take it. Also, my sales increased 76% percent. Michelle is the next Tony Robbins."

– J. Lewakowski

"I had been going through challenging experiences in my professional life, which were impacting me negatively in all areas of life--even inducing clinical depression...You are given the tools to "win" and succeed from now until forever."

– K. Sellers

"Michelle with IPV has done a great job working with our staff to develop much needed skills in time planning, managing personal stress, empathy, listening and many other skills. Her direct approach and dedication to helping people succeed has been a welcome resource for our team."

– J. Thomas

"Her skills are above bar; her instruction is engaging; her knowledge is wide-ranging, offering a wealth of information used to build one's self growth; and her compassion is contagious."

– B. Hines

"I found the tools she provided were essential to my personal growth, focus, and realization of the importance of time management. A worthwhile investment in myself."

– C. Krawczyk

"I feel so much more positive, optimistic, happy and driven to accomplish my goals! The encouragement, thoughtful accountability and incredible information she shared put me on the path to success and I now feel UNSTOPPABLE!"

– A. Criswell

"I have seen a dramatic positive change in how I view myself and the world...I highly recommend her...to anyone looking to know how to achieve success an take control of your own life."

– R. Rice

"She was specifically mentioned as the best part of the training program. She raises the productivity of those she is around."

– T. Lynema

"She will leave you in awe of the improvements to your team...their efficiency and productivity, their new and improved attitudes, their changed lives. Michelle is a leader of leaders."

– L. Lyons

"Michelle has a proven track record of success in her professional career and excels at building integrated high performing teams. She can work with any group of people and manage the process to optimize their performance, which is a gift that seems to come naturally to her."

– W. DeJong

YOUR JOURNEY TO
GREATNESS
THROUGH ROUTINE
A Guide to Creating a Success Routine

By Michelle L. Steffes

Never stop reaching higher!

Blessed Pen Ink Publishing

Blessed Pen Ink Publishing

Join us at **blessedpenink.com**

Write to inspire@blessedpenink.com

Printed in the United States of America

Blessed Pen Ink is a division of Meochia Nochi Blount Publishing

ISBN-10 0-9740777-3-9

ISBN-13 978-0-9740777-3-4

Cover, Jacket Design and Illustrations by Carolyn M. Steffes

Photography by Kristen Hernandez

While the author has made every effort to provide accurate telephone numbers, Internet addresses, and other contact information at the time of publication, neither the publisher nor the author assumes any responsibility of errors, or for changes that occur after publication. Further, the publisher does not have any control over and does not assume any responsibility for author or third-party websites or their content.

Except for friends and family, names and identifying characteristics of individuals mentioned have been changed to protect their privacy.

ACKNOWLEDGEMENT & DEDICATION

As I pen this page, so many people flash through my mind and touch my heart. I am certain the list would be far too long to include everyone who affected my "Journey to Greatness" in some way. There are those who inspired me and those who, through painful times in my journey, stirred up a raging fire within me to become more. I will begin with a few names worth mentioning and end with many "unnamed" who deserve to be acknowledged.

My first dedication goes out to the Lord of my life without whom, I would have never made it.

Next, I want to dedicate this book to Mark, James, Carolyn and Liz who have stood by me, encouraged me and supported me at every twist and turn in life. These are the pillars in my world!

For my Mother whom I love and cherish. Thank you for showing me how to grow through trials, stay true to myself and laugh at life.

For my Father (rest his soul). Thank you for teaching me to be bold and relentless in whatever I dreamt to become.

For my sisters Deb and Cheryl. Thank you for always believing in me.

For my mentor, Carla. Thank you for always being there to support me in challenges and celebrate me in victories. You have been a solid rock in my life and have given me more than I could ever thank you for.

For all of my clients throughout the years. While we walked together creating your journey to greatness, without you, I would be far less than I am today. You have enriched my life in many different ways. I cherish each one of you and so appreciate the opportunity you gave me to partner with you on your own journey. Special thanks to those clients who were willing to share their stories through the Case Studies in this book or to the testimonials listed inside.

For my truest friends (you know who you are). Thank you for your devotion and constant support.

For my editor/publisher, Meochia. You have been a joy and inspiration to work with!

Finally, to all those who desire to be more but have been beaten down by life. I dedicate this book to each and every one of you:

- *Those who have only known mediocrity but sense there is greatness in them.*
- *Those who have been "labeled" by others leaving scars on their hearts and doubt in their minds about who they really are.*
- *Those who know what they are capable of but just don't know how to make it happen.*
- *Those whom the world has tossed aside yet they have hope there is something greater out there for them*
- *Those who feel "stuck" in life or career and want to reach the next level but don't know where to begin.*
- *Those who have tried relentlessly to succeed but continually end up exasperated and back at square one.*

Love,
Michelle

TABLE OF CONTENTS

INTRODUCTION

Chances are you are reading this book because you know what you want out of life but may be a bit vague in areas about how to get there. Don't feel alone, I was right where you are once along with roughly 85% of the population, according to statistics.

I have spent over two decades building and leading teams, pouring into multitudes of clients and investing over 10,000 hours of personal study on the brain science behind habits and routines. I have discovered that there really is a pattern to developing greatness from within.

In my own journey, I was able to rebound from a serious career set back and double my new business in only six months. This happened as a result of creating a solid success routine and sticking to it. Furthermore, I have seen in myself and in my clients, dramatic changes in both personal and professional mindsets. These changes have restored relationships, massively increased income, produced multiple promotions, and created wholeness in mind and body along with many other benefits.

My style of helping people win is uniquely different as it paints a clear picture of what is happening inside your mind and body while taking you through a metamorphosis of complete change. Every step provided gives you the "why" behind the "what" so you can fully comprehend the science and psychological changes you are making. You will discover solid applications that transform old habits into brand new ways of thinking, acting and being.

With your desire to succeed, determination to win and passion for a better version of YOU, it is time to learn to how to build a new success routine that will equip you to alter your future forever! So get ready!

Get ready to get "unstuck" in your life or career!

Get ready to take your life from "okay" to "amazing"!

Get ready to overcome past regrets, hurts and old habits!

Learn the science of habits with practical insights, tools and steps to take in order to build your own personal "Success Routine". Whether you are seeking out new opportunities or restoring lost ones, the applications in this book are truly transformative.

Discover ways to retrain your brain, alter your physiology and expand your potential at many levels.

Be inspired by Case Studies in which others have accomplished Greatness through Routine and how they did it.

Realize the power of creating a Vision Statement (Chapter 2), the art of Cognitive Restructuring (Chapter 3), the necessity of Cognitive Consonance (Chapter 5), how to get Unstuck (Chapter 7), how to Master Energy, Focus and Time (Chapters 8 & 9), along with many other tools and applications to equip you for the Journey.

When you truly understand the science behind the mechanics of your brain and body chemistry, creating a new routine to produce who you want to become not only makes sense but it becomes very malleable and attainable.

Throughout this book, there is unique, science backed information and steps to take that will give you a brand new outlook on what life/career can be for you and a multitude of others. You will find brief Assignments, Downloadable Tools, Success Routine and Greatness Tips, Quotes, Charts, Resources and Routine Builders to empower you further.

Whether you are seeking to advance a successful career or struggling, there are solutions within this step-by-step guide to help raise the standard and take you to a level you have never been before and keep you there. So turn the page and begin now!

SECTION ONE – THE PSYCHOLOGY AND SCIENCE OF GREATNESS

CHAPTER ONE – FIRST STEPS

"If you always do what you've always done, you will always get what you've always got."

— Henry Ford

Real and lasting change cannot occur without addressing your daily routine. You must begin to take a hard look at your career and life choices from an entirely different perspective. It is the daily habits, rituals, mindsets and behaviors we choose, often without realizing it that can keep us from achieving our greatest potential.

Resolve to become a student of yourself by studying how you think, what you talk about and how you spend your time, personally and professionally. As you continue reading, you will discover the science behind this necessary training and you will get clear guidelines on how to accomplish it.

There is a case study for each chapter in the first section of this book, which includes actual clients. Although their names are changed, the stories are true. Each study proves how the impact of a routine for success can transform areas of your life faster than anything else you can do.

CASE STUDY #1

JEN'S STORY

It was around Christmas and Jen was feeling desperate for solutions. She felt passed over at least 3 times in her job of 27 years and her marriage was not what she dreamed it would be. Each day, almost mindlessly, she would simply "go through the motions". Her husband became depressed and often spoke of his unhappiness at work. He just couldn't seem to please his boss. In listening to his conversations, Jen feared he was on the brink of losing his job. She felt lost and began wondering if there was a future for her in both life and career.

She spent a lot of time reminiscing on how pleasurable life used to be. In her earlier years, she was jovial, fun and loved life! Now, life seemed to keep dealing her the same hand with the same monotonous results. She found herself struggling to get up in the morning just to face another predictable, drab day with no real purpose. Mornings would begin with hitting the snooze button multiple times and then rushing to prepare for her day under pressure. This daily routine filled her with thoughts of anxiety before even leaving home and remained with her in the drive to work.

In an effort to create some sort of fulfillment and purpose, Jen would often sign up for volunteering and other activities. In each attempt to fill the void in her life, the relentless inner dialogue of negative messages seemed to take over. They inhibited her ability to find any joy or fulfillment, even in doing well for others.

While at a volunteer event, Jen began sharing her frustrations with her friend, Tracy. In response, Tracy shared the recent changes she was making in her daily routine, what she was doing to create this new perspective on life, and how it was affecting her career. Tracy's changes caused her sales to rise more in four months' time than in her first three years combined. Jen was inspired!

Author's Note: You will discover what changes she made throughout the pages of this book. As you continue to read through, be certain to pause for every tip, question and assignment to learn how you can achieve great things by altering your routine.

Upon hearing the secret of Tracy's transformation, Jen felt a spark of hope and resolved to take the same actions.

In the beginning of her new journey, Jen discovered there were many changes she had to make in her daily routine and in her thought life. At first, it seemed daunting and a bit overwhelming but she stuck with the process. In a short amount of time, she recognized that the changes, although seemingly small, made a significant difference in her perceptions on life, relationships, career, success and even challenges. As she continued, she noticed joy returning to her life as the heavy weight of hopelessness and despair slowly lifted.

In just four weeks of remaining diligent to the changes in her routine, Jen's supervisor and others began asking about the difference in her, which continued to be the trend. This made her even more excited and hopeful about her future. Life became a joyous adventure once again.

Jen was convinced of this new revelation and resolved to remain consistent in developing her new success routine, permanently. Within three months, she received the task of launching an entirely new program for her workplace.

Even more amazing, Jen reconnected with her boss. Several months prior, they seemed disjointed and communication was difficult if not impossible. Jen reached out with compassion and respect, and began working on restoring that relationship. Due to her newfound confidence and boldness, she was able to present a well-written proposal and begin working on a project that would eventually transform the entire organization. She felt a greater and greater sense of value and purpose.

The new lifestyle Jen had adopted seemed to be affecting everyone in her path and it seemed as if her transformation was contagious. Even at home, things were evolving. Several weeks into her transformation, Jen's husband was still struggling with hardships at his job. It was sending him further into despair for his situation. While her life was taking a turn for the better, his life and career was in a downward spiral. Things began to shift fairly, quickly. With the changes in Jen and his second-hand exposure to her new routine, he was able to make the journey out of depression. Within two months, he was searching for a new occupation and eventually found a new and better job. Jen and her husband are now, both happily employed and excited about their future.

Today, Jen continues her new success routine and remains just as resolved to keep striving for daily growth. She now understands how to empower herself as she goes through each day with a completely different mindset and approach.

She received two promotions and initiated an entirely new program for the company. Jen is now an established Professional Development Director. She mediates for top leadership within her company and executive leadership has recognized her for her accomplishments. Jen has created a new life with all new perspectives. She is steadily increasing her potential in all aspects of life and career! And the best part? Jen is no longer "invisible" in her work environment or anywhere else! In her own words, she states, "I am no longer invisible but a force to be reckoned with!"

TAKE ONE STEP AT A TIME

Your first week should be dedicated to building your foundation. Progress is never made in an instant but through many intentional decisions and changes over a course of time.

- ✓ **DETERMINE**
- ✓ **BELIEVE**
- ✓ **APPLY**

Determine to set your heart in a direction that will daily prime you with new and fresh ideas.

Believe in your ability to achieve greatness

Apply the new perceptions you are committed to learning every day.

Don't let yourself get overwhelmed...take ONE STEP at a time. Just as in Jen's story, the greatest achievements result from the smallest of beginnings. Each small change you make, leads to big shifts in your life both professionally and personally.

The great news is that you can customize your new approach in a manner that will not interfere with your current obligations or commitments. Accomplish working on goals and inspiring change by exchanging the mundane for the purposeful.

There are many things we spend our valuable time on which could be considered mundane. Things such as Facebook, Twitter, Pinterest, emails, texts, television and many others can become useless distractions. If we are very honest about our schedules, we will discover opportunities to become more intentional about the way we live, how we think and who we become.

FIRST ASSIGNMENT:

Remove from your mind, all obstacles and inhibitions. Then write out who you wish to become and what goals you want to accomplish. Perform this task by forming three separate categories in your list making:

1. Personal Development

2. Professional Development

3. Material Goals or Gain

Then think carefully and prioritize the items in each list beginning with the one that will take you the farthest, the fastest.

Remember, you spend 8 hours sleeping and 8 hours working. This leaves you with 8 hours to work on your development and growth goals.

> **SUCCESS ROUTINE TIP #1:**
>
> Consider how you can rearrange your current routine. New habits are never developed by trying to "fit them in" with your old routine. There will never appear to be enough time. That is why we must create time for anything new.

Here are three examples of how to find time to develop new habits:

1

If you drive a meager 12,000 miles per year and you exchange what you currently listen to in the car with educational material, in 3 years it is equivalent to 2 years of college.

2

If you spend only 20 minutes per day reading topics of interest, it equates to 20, 200-page books per year. Choosing to work on yourself instead of watching TV or spending time on social media is only one of many ways you can create drastic change.

3

If you want to adopt an exercise routine, you could awake 20-30 minutes earlier. In time, you would become accustomed to rising earlier and you would begin enjoying the benefits. In fact, you would alter your physiology (body chemistry) creating an addiction to your new morning routine.

SUCCESS IS A JOURNEY

John Maxwell and Brian Tracy are two highly successful authors, speakers and teachers both create winning routines. Each set goals, stays persistent and keep moving forward. Both, Maxwell and Tracy, tell us, "Success is a Journey, not a destination."

The definition of Journey according to Dictionary.com is traveling from one place to another, usually taking a rather long time; trip or passage or progress from one stage to another.

That's why it is important to remember that every day, you are either moving forward or backward based on the actions you are taking but you are never just sitting still.

When we think we are just sitting still, we actually put ourselves in a position of compromise. In this state, we will NEVER make any headway. Realistically, in this position, we are actually moving backwards in our progress because of our stagnancy.

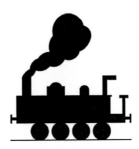

Imagine your success journey as a train. Unless you begin pouring in coal or wood, the train will never have the energy to move to its next destination. The actions for growth you take each day are the coal or fuel. How far or how fast you travel is completely in your hands.

Taking responsibility for our own success and progress always begins with us. Regardless of where we are right now and what has happened to us, we can choose to pour on the coal and start moving forward. On the other hand, we can choose to blame others, make excuses or find reasons why we are not moving. Even in cases where we may have been betrayed, rejected or mistreated, it is still up to us. Until we decide to pick up the shovel and begin putting in our own coal, we will never see progress.

It is important to remember that everyone has a story to tell. Everyone has been hurt, treated unfairly or damaged at some point in our lives. It is not about what goes on outside of us as much as what goes on inside of us.

With each day that you choose to take action, you will **raise the standard** in your life. Determine to change your daily habits and see opportunities instead of struggles. By this, you will increasingly experience more of the following as you progress:

- ✓ **Deeper Inner Peace and Confidence**

- ✓ **Certainty about your abilities and your future**

- ✓ **Creativity and Vigor on the job**

- ✓ **Clarity and Direction**

- ✓ **Excitement and Zeal about overcoming new challenges**

- ✓ **Resolve and Determination to see your vision fulfilled**

- ✓ **Improved Health; mentally, emotionally, spiritually and physically**

Human physiology teaches that when we allow fear or stress to overcome us, two hormones are released, adrenaline and cortisol. Adrenaline is a superpower of sorts and it is typically the reason people indulge in extreme sports or horror movies. The "high" they experience from the adrenaline rush can be addictive. In cases of true emergencies or life-threatening circumstances, adrenaline provides surges of power that are somewhat super-human in nature.

However, to the level we allow stress or fear to overtake us on a day to day, the same amount of cortisol will be released. When this happens, it will paralyze portions of the frontal lobe in our brains. This frontal lobe is referred to as "the executive center". The entire response is called, "fight or flight."

In situations where we are authentically in danger, the release of these chemicals can be lifesaving. Think of the mother whose child is trapped under a car in an accident. She will do anything to save her child. She runs over, picks up the car, almost effortlessly, and pulls her child to safety. She was able to do so because of the supernatural strength provided by the adrenaline. At the same time, the cortisol paralyzed the reasoning portion of her frontal cortex so that she would not consider the fact that she cannot pick up a car. This is also true regarding soldiers on the battlefield or when we are threatened and need to make decisions without time for reasoning. However, if cortisol is allowed to remain in our brains too long or at levels that are too high, it can create a life of senseless self-destruction, with the debilitating symptoms of chronic stress.

SYMPTOMS OF CHRONIC STRESS

- ☐ Inadequate sleep

- ☐ Poor eating habits

- ☐ Emotional distress

- ☐ Reduced attention

- ☐ Decreased perception (Brain Fog)

- ☐ Loss of short-term memory

- ☐ Reduced learning receptivity and retention

- ☐ Difficulty communicating, clearly

THESE SYMPTOMS ARE A RESULT OF:

- ✓ Decreased regulation of cortisol

- ✓ Increases in glucocorticoids

- ✓ Cellular changes in the hippocampus

* Source: Women's Health Network

TOP 10 STRESS RELATED ILLNESSES*

1. Heart Disease

2. Asthma

3. Obesity

4. Diabetes

5. Headaches

6. Depression

7. Reflux & IBS

8. Alzheimer's

9. Accelerated Aging

10. Premature Death

Source: WebMD.com

WHO OR WHAT IS IN CONTROL?

I have found there are two major indicators or red flags that reveal when we are not in control, anxiety and frustration.

Each of these are a sign that we are either not choosing to empower ourselves with a daily routine which creates positive mindsets OR we are simply succumbing to the dictates of our circumstances around us. In other words, we are living reactively instead of intentionally.

An estimated 80-85% of the population lives "reactively".

When we are reactive, our responses are controlled by what I often refer to as a "two-year-old" mindset.

We respond to every situation, neglecting the power we have to control how we respond. We are manipulated by our own feelings in the moment; we do not take time to be emotionally intelligent about what is really happening or how we want the outcome to be. Unless we take back control, this pattern will resurface every time we face challenges making us a "run-away" from our opportunities for growth and advancement. *It's time to take back control!*

ROUTINE BUILDERS FROM CHAPTER ONE

1. Evaluate your current daily routine. List habits which are time "wasters" or time spent that may be inhibiting your growth:

_____

_____

_____

_____

2. Exchange the mundane for the purposeful in your everyday life or career. List new habits you would like to adopt in replacement of those listed in #1:

_____

_____

_____

_____

3. From the habits in #2, list tasks you must schedule into your daily routine and prioritize them in order of importance:

_____

_____

_____

_____

GREATNESS TIP 1: To develop a new Success Routine, you must be open to altering your current schedule.

GREATNESS TIP 2: Managing your schedule to be more productive and fulfilling is the first step in reducing daily stress. As you design your lists, resolve to choose only tasks and activities that will give you a sense of daily purpose and progress.

CHAPTER TWO –

THE BRAIN

SCIENCE BEHIND

HABITS

Understanding some basic knowledge of brain functions and the neuroscience behind forming habits empowers you to take action with less reservation. When you become aware of cognitive response, you realize how plausible it is to re-wire or retrain your brain, creating new neural pathways and ultimately new mindsets. The only caveat is your willingness and determination to persist no matter how you may feel or what circumstances try to dissuade you. Most of us have heard that we can alter a mindset within 21-30 days. Interestingly, this philosophy stems from "neuroplasticity" which will be explained throughout this chapter.

Almost 95% of your daily decisions, actions, feelings and beliefs come from your subconscious mind, according to numerous cognitive studies performed over many decades. Your subconscious mind is actually 30,000 times more powerful than your conscious mind!

Over the course of your lifetime, many ideas, thoughts, beliefs and skills have entered into your mind creating new neural pathways and networks. These neural networks are the composition of your sub-conscious. The process of growing neural pathways and networks has been going on since your conception.

Your neurons begin growing "dendrites" each time you are exposed to something new. A dendrite is a pinkish-brown, protein substance that will grow and lengthen until it connects with the axon of another neuron.[1] This process occurs because of electrical impulses in the brain targeting specific sections of neurons often based on previous beliefs or concepts. From infancy to adulthood,

---

[1] http://www.human-memory.net/brain_neurons.html

each time we learn something new, we are creating new connections.[2] Each connection is called a synaptic connection. An adult brain over the age of 35 can have as many as one thousand-trillion synaptic connections.[3]

Networks of neural pathways are related. They determine how we think, how we process and how we perceive the world around us. The more thoughts you have about a particular subject, idea, issue or skill, the more neural connections will form, creating multiple networks in your brain bent in each direction. Whether positive or negative, you have built every network in your brain over a lifetime. Think of the many influences you are exposed to including ideals, education, tragedies, people and things. In many cases, if something tragic happened in our past, we grew a large network in that area due to thinking on it for weeks, months, years and even decades.

Another determining factor for large neural networks is memories that are vivid and painful. When strong emotions are involved, floods of hormones are released leaving a powerful "imprint" with deep roots that are difficult to extinguish. For each negative or positive neural network you create, your perception on life, success, wealth, work, people, religion, etc. is dramatically affected. The good news is that we can alter or transform those networks in the same manner they were created.

Who do you want to be? What do you want to do, have or accomplish? Whatever new information you determine to program into your subconscious must begin with a change in your

---

[2] Brain World Magazine, September 30, 2017 – Neuroplasticity: Experience and Your Brain
[3] http://www.human-memory.net/brain_neurons.html

daily thoughts. The easiest and most effective way to produce a new thought life is through a change in daily habits.

> *"Guard your Heart with all diligence for out of it flow the Issues of Life!"*
>
> Proverbs 4:23

Remember, you did not create the negative neural networks overnight, so you will not alter them overnight. Although it takes 21-30 days to begin the necessary changes in perceptions, it can take up to 3 cycles or 63-90 days to develop into a sustained habit.[4] In cases where the networks deeply connect with many other networks, it can take much longer to alter. Real and lasting change requires long-term commitment with constant and consistent changes over an extended period of time.

If you are willing to follow through with the suggestions made in this book and commit to retraining your brain daily, dramatic changes can be made at an accelerated pace. In fact, for those networks, which are recent, you may find it quicker and easier to create desired changes. Networks that began much earlier in life can take much longer to reverse and finally transform.

Case after case, proves that ALL networks (e.g., habits) can change if you are willing to stay with it regardless of how long takes.

---

[4] Switched on Brain by Caroline Leaf

CASE STUDY #2

TOM'S STORY

After devoting 26 years to working in public service, Tom was at a crossroads in his life and career. His children were almost grown and he had a desire to do something greater.

In the fall, he was required to attend mandatory staff training. He assumed it would be something he heard before. He did not realize that what he was about to hear would change his life forever.

I was commissioned to provide a two-day training for the city's entire civil servant team. The topic was "Resilience in Times of Change". The core of this training evolved around brain science and altering old mindsets. Tom learned that through daily subtle, yet powerful changes in his routine and habits, he could completely alter his destiny. He was riveted and enticed to the point of seeking additional information. Soon he requested a discussion about how he could acquire help in creating the change he was so hungry for. This was the beginning of a brand-new journey of discovery and growth for him.

The first thing Tom was required to do was develop a personal vision statement along with five specific goals to take him there. His decision was easy. Tom immediately set a goal of achieving a very prestigious position in a year's time. It seemed like a very steep goal but he really wanted it for himself, his family and his community. Furthermore, he was committed to the process and willing to put in the work to make it happen.

The next step was to begin putting together a customized success routine that would take him there.

Day after day, Tom worked diligently adopting new habits that would serve to "retrain his brain". He also worked hard on the relationships in his personal and professional life. He desired to engage with them more deeply and show more compassion. The more he succeeded at making an impact in his relationships, the more driven he became to take his new routine to the next level and the easier it seemed to get. After a couple of weeks, others began noticing dramatic and wonderful changes in Tom, too.

One of the important things Tom had to learn was sowing and reaping, sometimes referred to as "karma" or the "law of attraction." This phenomenon is present for all of us whether we acknowledge it or not. In other words, we will either attract opportunities for ourselves or keep them away based on the impact we make, good or bad, in our world around us.

Three weeks into his efforts towards massive change, a new position he was hoping for within travel distance of his home opened up, unexpectedly. Tom was beside himself in considering the possibilities. It was all happening so much faster than he predicted. With some coaxing and encouraging, he took a chance and pursued the opportunity.

Although the application process was tedious and time consuming, he was patient. Sticking to his new success routine made him feel confident and bold.

After weeks of waiting, it was announced that he was in the top three of over 40 nationwide candidates for the position. This seemed too good to be true... Even his family felt it was surreal. It was not over yet. He still had to pass through two more processes and to Tom, his competition seemed much more qualified. The pressure was intense. He struggled with the overwhelming task of juggling the obligations of his current position while continuing through the application process. Had it not been for his diligence to the success routine he had adopted, he may have choked under the pressure.

The next day, the news he had been waiting for came in. Tom won the position and was beside himself with gratitude! He paused for a moment to look back and realized that all of this had taken place in only five weeks! He was amazed at what he accomplished and who he became to his family, friends and community. The position he set his sights to win in one year, he now held in just over a month.

Tom discovered that the key to his success was more about WHO he had become than what his circumstances had led him to.

The routine that Tom adopted is one that anyone is capable of and the results can be just as amazing!

THE KEY TO TRANSFORMATION – SYNAPTIC PRUNING

The next principle we need to discuss in order to fully understand the brain science of habits is a powerful key in the cause and effect of transformation. This key is found in a term called "synaptic pruning" which is an important part of Neural Plasticity, a term we mentioned earlier.

Synaptic pruning is a process in which the brain will literally shed or eliminate older, weakened neural synaptic connections. These are typically connections that are no longer used or are superseded by new information, which negates old beliefs or ideals held. In this process, the old, useless pathways will literally fall off the neuron making room for new connections.

Here's a simple example to help you understand how this process works:

Let's say you travel to Europe to stay for 30 days. If you are from the Western world, you will have to learn how to drive on the left side of the road instead of the right.

At first, it will seem incredibly awkward and somewhat terrifying. However, after approximately three weeks of daily driving it will become more natural to you.

Why? Because your brain has stopped the electrical impulses from "feeding" the neural pathways containing the data which programmed you to drive on the right side of the road.

At the same time, your brain developed new neural pathways to program you to drive on the left side.

Upon returning to your homeland in the west, you will find yourself feeling awkward all over again because you must reverse the entire process. The only difference you may find is that since your deepest connections or networks are developed in driving on the right, reversing the synaptic connections will take less time and seem easier than when you were in Europe learning to adopt a new habit for the very first time.

An interesting take away in this example is that you will likely feel quite awkward when first beginning a new habit or success routine for change. This is why the majority of the population will give up on New Year's Resolutions within two weeks. If we are to accomplish real change, we will have to commit to daily change over a minimum of three weeks before noticing any convincing results.

As with Tom's story, when we are intentional about changing our habits and daily routines, determining to stay with it no matter what it takes, we will watch our greatest dreams unfold before our very eyes. The types of changes we must be willing to make in order to retrain our brain consist of things like what we listen to, think about and pay attention to. It is only when we become cognizant of what influences us that we can drastically transform our minds to conceive new perceptions. The same phenomenon occurs when we are learning a new skill, studying for a new occupation or challenging ourselves with new knowledge. The brain will respond in the same manner when our eyes are opened to a philosophy or a truth that we were formerly incorrect about due to wrong suppositions or poor influences of our past.

SECOND ASSIGNMENT:

Take the goals you wrote down in chapter one and write out a vision statement for yourself by condensing it down into one or two sentences. Make sure it starts with "I am". Then start paying attention to everything you allow into your thought life; writing down ideas on how you can feed your subconscious thoughts that will align with your vision.

Deliberately choose philosophies, education and concepts that push you forward and keep you on track. Put your vision on small cards so you can refer to it and speak it out often. Study it as if you were taking an exam you absolutely must pass. It will require discipline at first but real changes start to become obvious within 21-30 days, after which, it gets a bit easier. Results depend upon how diligent you are to make decisive and significant alterations in your routine. Your statement will help you determine if your choices in activities are moving you forward or holding you back from seeing your vision to fruition.

For a Vision Mapping Tool and full instructions on how to create a Personal Vision Statement, visit:

http://greatnessthroughroutine.com

SUCCESS ROUTINE TIP #2:

When writing your vision, think about four strengths you possess that will get you to your ultimate destination in life or career. Under each strength write out four of each; goals you want to work on and resources that will aid you in the process.

Taking inventory will give you a clearer picture of how much you really have going for you. It will also reveal capabilities or resources you forgot about or laid aside.

THE SCHOOL OF SUCCESS

As with anything you want to grow in, it will require a sacrifice of your time and energy

- ✓ If we determine to lose weight, we will have to change our eating habits and lifestyle

- ✓ If we want to gain a degree in college, it requires us to apply ourselves diligently, taking time for classes, studies and exams

- ✓ If we want job promotions, we have to work hard, learn our position well and go the extra mile

- ✓ Try to look at this endeavor as a "school of success". If you want to take your life and your career to the next level, you will need to

- ✓ Be deliberate and methodical in managing your time

- ✓ Stay committed to daily learning and growth

✓ Set measurable goals and take steps to complete them

✓ Develop a vision and use it to keep your focus

✓ Be open to changing or adding new habits and routines

✓ Maintain a resolve to Do Whatever it Takes!

The whole process begins when you "feed your brain" exactly what it needs to grow and avoid those things that cause it to feel fearful, doubtful or uncertain. One philosophy I find very useful in doing whatever it takes is to keep telling myself, "If you are too comfortable, you are not growing."

Like the earlier example about driving in Europe, if we are truly honest with ourselves, we can look back and see that those uncomfortable moments in life are where we find the most growth.

Years ago, I was at a crossroads in my career forcing me to make some very difficult decisions about my own success routine. Just like Tom, I wanted to take my career to the next level and financially, I just had to. I was working morning until night trying to pull all the pieces together to make it happen. I had made some progress but it just wasn't happening fast enough. Furthermore, the progress I did make seemed meager for the efforts I was putting forth. Thoughts of doubt and fear constantly badgered me as I pushed on utilizing my experience, education and raw willpower on a day to day to bring about some kind of success.

There finally came a day of decision for me. On that day, I clenched my fists, gritted my teeth and said to myself, "No More! I will not lose one more thing! I am going to do whatever it takes, no matter what it costs me!"

That was the decision that influenced me to start looking at my routine, habits and vision from a different perspective. I was no longer "just interested" in going to the next level, I was committed. This mind shift is the foundation for drastic change.

At that point, I began a "Morning Power Hour" that altered my state of mind and infused me with a sort of "super power" which became the foundation to multiplying my business by 200% in less than six months!

MY MORNING POWER HOUR

Building a brand-new routine takes discipline, commitment and perseverance.

When I first developed the morning portion of my success routine, I determined to wake up an hour and a half earlier each day (4:30am) and create my own "power hour" filled with exercise, prayer, affirmations and insightful podcasts. The mental exercise prepared me to start my day with an outstanding mind set, while the physical exercise empowered my brain and body to become more alert, creative and clear. Within a few weeks, I noticed more energy to tackle the day as well as relief from brain fatigue and brain fog.

Both physical and biological evidence proves that physical exercise triggers the pituitary gland, which then floods our bodies and our brains with endorphins. This produces an "energized mental high".

In fact, studies find that a good dose of endorphins can be 200 times more powerful than morphine. (This is covered in greater detail in later chapters.)

In the beginning, it was not easy for me at all. For the first month, I stood sleepy-eyed in the bathroom arguing with myself and wanting to go back to bed. Sometimes, I even succumbed to the temptation, convincing myself that sleep was more important.

After approximately four weeks of persistence, I began to really notice a difference and my "why" (vision) became bigger and bigger. The combination of my "why' and the new habit that was now forming helped me stay determined to stick with it despite how I was feeling on any particular morning.

This is how I was able to increase my business by 200% in such a small about of time. Years later, I still keep this incredibly valuable routine, Monday through Friday, every week and I love it!

Never give up. The payoff is worth it!

What do you do when you arise in the morning? What time do you start your day? Do you find the beginning of your day energizing and positive or hurried and negative? Perhaps it's time for a change.

ROUTINE BUILDERS FROM CHAPTER TWO

1. Your thoughts are built up into negative and positive neural networks over a lifetime. Consider taking a 48-hour Thought Diary Challenge. Use the lines below or a journal to record the types of thoughts that run through your mind most of the time:

_____

_____

_____

_____

_____

_____

_____

_____

2. In Chapter One, you were asked to create new habits for managing your time more effectively and intentionally. The same can be said of your thoughts. Take a few moments to list out some things in your life or career that you can and should be happy about. Now challenge yourself to cultivate the positive instead of the negative:

_____

_____

_____

_____

_____

_____

_____

GREATNESS TIP 3: Writing your personal Vision Statement will empower you with focus and clarity.

GREATNESS TIP 4: Managing your mind to focus on things that make you feel grateful or accomplished is the next step in reducing daily stress. As you design days into constructive thinking, resolve to choose only activities and entertainment that will push you forward into your destiny.

CHAPTER THREE—

RETRAINING YOUR BRAIN THROUGH COGNITIVE RESTRUCTURING

Retraining your brain from a lifetime of wrong perceptions not only requires a success routine but "tools" to empower you daily and aid you in keeping your focus. There are many useful tools to help you move from level to level while staying the course.

Altering your neural pathways and ultimately your mindsets from a lifetime of harmful thinking requires cognitive restructuring. The practice of cognitive restructuring can accelerate the process as you learn how to alter your perceptions. It is also a powerful foundation in Cognitive Behavioral Therapy, a practice often used by counselors to reverse negative tendencies in their patients. Below is a helpful four-step guide to cognitive restructuring. For a printable worksheet, visit:

http://greatnessthroughroutine.com

THIRD ASSIGNMENT –
Four-Step Guide to Cognitive Restructuring

Step #1: Write a recent occurrence that produced negative thoughts, fear, apprehension, or anxiety for you.

Step #2: Record the negative thoughts you had at the time of the situation or event.

Step #3: Remove yourself from all emotional ties to the event as well as any presuppositions, and then write in a few rational observations.

Step #4: Consider a list of positive responses you can choose to apply based on the rational observation in step #3.

Situation/Event	Negative Thoughts	Rational Observation	Positive Response

Another powerful tool I recommend in any success routine is daily affirmations. I am not referring to simply repeating a few positive statements every day. When you merely think or speak positively but you have no solid belief about it; or what you are saying does not agree with your core or inner beliefs, it will accomplish nothing. This kind of mental posture is known as, "cognitive dissonance". It was first mentioned in earlier chapters but now, we will dive deeper into what it means.

Affirmations can only be an effective form of cognitive restructuring when there is "cognitive consonance", which Businessdictionary.com defines as a state of harmony and internal consistency arising from compatibility among a person's attitudes, behavior, beliefs, and/or knowledge. Opposite of cognitive dissonance.

Therefore, simply speaking affirmations is not enough to create change. You must speak affirmations AS IF you truly believe, using your mind, heart and emotions. When you first begin using affirmations, you will likely be dealing with a mixture of cognitive consonance and cognitive dissonance, making the process difficult and seemingly useless at times. However, when you engage all three simultaneously with visualization, you powerfully influence your neural pathways even at their deepest level.

Affirmations reinforced, frequently and consistently, will eventually persuade your heart and mind to come into agreement with your core values and align with what you are saying.

At this point, you may be asking, "So how does cognitive restructuring make things happen in the exterior world around me?" To answer that question, I refer to another great proverb which states, "As a man thinks in his heart, so is he." Proverbs 23:7

Think for a moment about someone that you know who is wealthy or successful. Now think about the types of people and opportunities they currently attract to them. What if they awoke one day and started thinking they were poor and struggling at life, relationships and in their career? If they persisted down this path and began making decisions that aligned with this new belief system, over time, it would it change who was attracted to them and eventually ruin their financial state.

In the same way, we can be certain that how we dress, act, speak, think and live will affect who we attract, what opportunities come our way and whether or not we see our goals to fruition.

Do you still struggle with this philosophy? Let's look at a real statistic:

According to the National Endowment for Financial Education, "about 70 percent of people who suddenly receive a windfall of cash will lose it within a few years."

The reason for this sad fact is that they have not developed their mindsets to cope with large amounts of money. They are in cognitive dissonance at so many levels causing them to make devastating and uninformed decisions with their fortune. In effect, they are trying to take a short cut to riches without changing who they are in their subconscious.

Remember, the subconscious is the place in our minds where neural connections are the strongest. Therefore, instead gaining finances, they end up losing it all and more.

CASE STUDY #3

KIM'S STORY

Kim had a strong desire to make a difference in the lives of others. In her life and work, she demonstrated excellence. In fact, others would often refer to her as an "overachiever".

Kim worked for an organization that was quite involved with the public eye on many levels. Her position required her to spend many hours creating opportunities to interact and build relationships with the community. She was also accountable to the leadership team so her name was well known within the organization and she established herself quite well.

After 7 years of dedicated work, the winds of favor shift for Kim. This was confusing to her because in her mind, she did all she could to maintain a strong and influential rapport. She was always conscientious of how she presented herself to leadership and the community.

However, there seemed to be a growing resentment or perhaps even jealousy forming between her and some of the leaders in the organization.

Despite her efforts to be cooperative and kind, it seemed matters only became worse. Soon, it became evident that she was allowing the tension in the atmosphere to get inside her causing mental anguish and distress. Every effort she made to keep peace and do her job seemed futile.

Kim decided she would need help from outside of her work environment to regain her confidence, which was broken from months of unmerited pressure towards her.

She attended an event for women where she heard a message I shared on "Avoiding Burnout". Since she felt she was on the fringes of burnout herself, the entire presentation resonated with her. What seemed to stand out the most was the information she heard about retraining your brain and altering your subconscious to become more resilient. The appeal of this concept stayed with her so she reached out to me immediately after the event. She wanted to find out if this was real and discover what she needed to do to retrain her brain.

After a brief discussion, she knew it was an easy decision.

In short order, Kim began her new journey of altering her perceptions, changing her routines and improving her inner dialogue. Within the first week of her brain training, she noticed a gradual but significant return of her confidence levels. After two weeks, others began to inquire about where she was getting this sudden inner-strength and sense of well-being. Some in her department knew of the injustices done to her and were very happy for her as she continued to rediscover her strength. Others, who were spiteful of her before, only dug their heels in more and made more attempts to bring her down.

Despite the animosity she was up against, she continued in her new success routine and in her resolve to be the best version of herself she could be. She fulfilled every request and assignment given to her with excellence and integrity. Kim also worked hard at empowering others and demonstrated kindness to everyone on the team.

In the end, she was let go. Instead of feeling devastated, she was strangely relieved and content. She knew she maintained her state of mind through it all and left with dignity.

She then began utilizing her gifts and influence along with her newfound strength and resilience to build the business of her dreams.

Today, Kim is empowering others to win and her new business is consistently growing. She recently launched an online video broadcast that spotlights the success of others and reports positive local news. She often reflects about how far she has come, "I thank God for the important changes in my routine during some of the most difficult weeks of my life. Changes that propelled me forward and altered my destiny."

Kim learned that empowering others always begins with empowering ourselves to win and no one can take that from her.

A DEEPER LOOK AT THE SUBCONSCIOUS MIND

Our subconscious is the entire infrastructure of neural networks that we have created since birth. With each new network, our perceptions and behavior are affected. Some of the deepest and most influential networks in our minds developed out of tragedy or traumatic events.

Think about where you were when something horribly tragic happened in your life. The magnitude of that event mixed with the feelings you felt and the consequences that most likely followed etched into your subconscious forever. It can be played back clearly in the theatre of your mind whenever prompted. The strong feelings you had at that time are what created such powerful memories. Compound that with thoughts that you most likely meditated on for days, weeks, months or even years after the tragedy and you have created significant changes in your mindsets, sometimes even altering your core values.

In the same way, if we want to create positive thoughts, images and beliefs about any one thing, we must first alter our subconscious mind. We do this by generating passion or emotion combined with thought in order to create the right neural pathways and sear new perceptions into our subconscious mind.

For years, athletes have trained using this concept. They are asked to visualize themselves competing in the sport of their choice, in their minds eye only, while hooked up to monitors. They must engage emotions, thoughts, feelings and other senses, i.e. sights, sounds, smells, feelings and even the outcome they desire.

These devices track their vital signs as well as their nerves and muscles. Amazingly, their vitals and muscle fibers react as if they were actually playing the sport itself. Study after study proves that the performance of an athlete improves vastly and consistently with this type of visualization.

Another example to consider is how your body reacts when you watch a horror movie or love story. Your heart rate speeds up; you may sweat, tense up or even cry. All because your thoughts are aligning with what is played on the screen. This type of scientific study concluded that the subconscious mind does not know the difference between an imagined event and an actual event.

The New England Journal of Medicine cites a case of placebo knee surgery involving 165 patients with osteoarthritis. These patients were randomly divided into separate groups set to undergo different procedures to study the results of each. Each group provided consent to participate in this study. We will call them Groups A and B.

Group A would have standard knee surgery. Group B would have placebo knee surgery in which 3 incisions, 1cm long, were made in the knee and then stitched up but no procedure was done. Patients in both groups were monitored for 24 months, collecting data in 3-month intervals. The results were conclusive indicating both groups experienced full recovery of the knee disorder.[5]

---

[5] https://www.nejm.org/doi/full/10.1056/NEJMoa013259

This study and multitudes of others reveal that what you perceive in your subconscious is the dominating factor in the outcome. Therefore, utilizing this knowledge as you pursue new habits and develop your success routine can only help. Realize that you are designed to succeed. You have the power to determine your outcome. All you have to do is tap into the resources you were born with.

To assist you in the cognitive restructuring required to alter your subconscious, I am including a copy of the affirmations I use every day and offer to my clients. Download at:

http://greatnessthroughroutine.com

Speak these affirmations WITH FEELING over yourself, twice daily for a minimum of 30 days. Be certain to personalize them with specifics that bring more meaning and definite vision to each one.

There is POWER in "I AM"

I am blessed	I am secure	I am the right weight
I am prosperous	I am disciplined	I am filled with gratitude
I am calm	I am focused	I am compassionate
I am healthy	I am attractive	The right people are in my future
I am talented	I am valuable	The right opportunities are headed my way
I am creative	I am well-liked	This is my year
I am confident	I am fun to be around	Great things are going to happen to me!
I am an overcomer	I have favor	This is my day!

SUCCESS ROUTINE TIP #3:

Just as your body needs healthy meals each day to maintain optimum performance, your mind requires the same. As you set up your new routine, try not to look at the changes as changes. Instead, view your new "mind diet" as a necessary discipline to achieving the end result. Your mind, just like your body, will underperform with a consistent diet of "junk food" such as TV, media, gossip, negative words, etc.

"Those who fail typically focus on the pain of change more than the end result."

Tony Robbins

ROUTINE BUILDERS FROM CHAPTER THREE

1. Cognitive Restructuring is a powerful way to alter bad perceptions and retrain your brain. What are some mindsets that seem to block you from the right perceptions?

_____

_____

_____

_____

_____

_____

_____

_____

_____

_____

_____

_____

_____

_____

GREATNESS TIP 5: Ponder the mindsets you desire to change. Start thinking about tools that you can equip yourself with daily to begin setting your vision in motion.

CHAPTER FOUR— THE GARDEN OF YOUR MIND

You have approximately 60,000 thoughts per day. In the Garden of Your Mind, are you tending to Weeds or Seeds?

WEEDS

- ✓ Rehearsing the Problem
- ✓ Un-Forgiveness
- ✓ Self-Pity
- ✓ Entitlement
- ✓ Taking Offense
- ✓ Comparing Yourself to Others
- ✓ Feeling Inadequate
- ✓ No Vision – No Goals
- ✓ Feeling Stuck

SEEDS

- ✓ Brush the "Dust" Off and Move Forward
- ✓ Forgive Yourself and Others
- ✓ Take Responsibility for Your Own Success
- ✓ Ignore the Critics
- ✓ Get a Coach or Mentor to Hold You Accountable
- ✓ Motivate & Grow Every Day
- ✓ Create a Personal Vision & Set Specific Goals

✓   Empower Others Often

You were born with approximately one-hundred billion neurons in your brain and forty-thousand in your heart; each designed to process and store information you provide. Just as in a garden, there are healthy plants and there are thorns and weeds (as listed in the beginning of this chapter). Even if you manage to create change in your perceptions and ultimately, your subconscious, you will have to maintain it every day for the rest of your life.

CASE STUDY #4

JOHN'S STORY

John began his career excited about life and filled with anticipation for a great future! At a fairly young age, he began living the American dream. He married, had children and quickly advanced up the ladder of success in his chosen career, grossing over 6 million in commissions in less than 10 years. At first, his world revolved around his marriage and his children, celebrating rich moments with them and enjoying the happy life they shared.

Over time, his career consumed him. It seemed the things that were once important to him began to fade in significance, due to the busyness of life and work. Unknowingly, John tailored his daily routines to conform to this busy lifestyle. In his mind, all in his life was good. Each day he would pour himself into his career without much thought about his state of mind or the health of his family relationships. He ignored all the warning signs.

Whenever, John was confronted with any opposition to his lifestyle, he simply justified it by reasoning within himself that it was normal and responsible behavior. He felt secure in the idea that he was working hard in order to provide for his family. Despite the continual requests from both his wife and his children for genuine attention, John just couldn't seem to find the time. The efforts he did make were somewhat disconnected and brief, resulting in a growing chasm between his family and the relationship they once shared.

The day came when his family walked out of his life. For John, it was shock and disbelief! He created multiple mindsets, which in effect, blinded him to the reality of what was really happening.

The break up was no surprise to his wife and children but it did not ease the pain for anyone.

Over the next several years, John's life continued to spin out of control. He now had to deal with the pain of losing what was most precious to him and the confusion of how he got to this place. With each passing year, John grew more discouraged and somewhat bitter, blaming events and people from his past for his misfortune.

In his brokenness and crushed state of mind, he adopted many new habits as a way to cope and survive. Some of them drove him further away from who he once knew himself to be which led to even more problems. Every area of his life was on a downward spiral.

In time, John realized how far he had fallen from the confident, successful man he once was. He reconciled with himself to reach out for help. One day he read a story online about someone who found victory through deliberate changes in their routine and their perceptions on life and career. He was inspired and new hope arose in his heart. He determined to act quickly, mustering up the courage to take the necessary steps to begin a new life once again.

At the beginning of his new journey, he was completely overwhelmed and even a bit discouraged. It was just too much to take in. Changes he needed to make in his daily routine seemed very difficult to him and he was afraid it would only end in more disappointment. At the same time, he knew he needed to do something drastic and take a chance. He resolved it was worth finding out if these changes would bring him the new life that he was looking for.

There were times he felt as if he was not accomplishing much. He was even frustrated with himself for his lack of discipline.

However, things started turning around. In a few short weeks, he found himself slowly adapting to a more conducive type of routine and lifestyle. Each day he put forth effort, he created new hope. As he persisted to stay on track with his newfound success routine, he grew stronger and more determined than ever to regain what he lost.

John had developed so many deeply rooted mindsets that set him back making many days seemed uphill to him. Yet, he persevered.

After five weeks of persisting, John began to see new signs of life in his finances, his health, his relationships and himself. In his own words he stated, "For the first time in years, I can see the light at the end of the tunnel."

Even after two years, John shared the following statement: "My past, decisions, how I saw myself and the issues I've had with acceptance and rejection, possibly enhanced by my adoption experience has kept me, in life, from being all I really am to and for others. That began to change two years ago as I began to declare every day and every time that I saw this (my vision) on my bathroom mirror, by my bed, by my workout apparatus, living room chair, refrigerator, kitchen cabinets, office desk, and wallet. [They] have all served as reminders of who I really am in Christ.

It's now becoming evident to the outside who I have truly been inside all my life, I pray and believe."

After 10 years, John has overcome several obstacles in his world. He rebuilt his health and pushed himself to get back on track in life. He clearly understands the importance of maintaining priorities, sticking to his new Success Routine and keeping a strong state of mind. He also realizes his journey is for life and to the degree he is willing to stay committed is the degree of success he will obtain.

John discovered that being aware of the weeds in our garden is never enough; we must take action daily to pull those weeds and replace them with good seeds on a daily basis. Only then, can we rise above and win!

No matter how many weeds you pull, a garden will always need tending to in order to produce a bountiful harvest. In the same manner, it will always be your responsibility to do whatever you can to keep out or extinguish those thorns and weeds before they can grow. Once they are large enough, they will inevitably choke out even those healthy networks you worked hard to grow.

The "garden of your mind" must never be left unattended. No matter how healthy the garden may seem, there will always be opportunities to allow weeds and thorns to creep in and bring destruction. When this happens, you can experience everything from poor health to depression and emotional upheaval affecting your career, relationships, well-being and success.

"Whatever a man sows, he will reap in return."

Galatians 6:7

Sowing good seeds to produce a healthy garden in your mind and heart must be considered from multiple perspectives. The changes in your routine and habits will always affect your inner thought life for better or for worse.

Now that you have your vision written, look at just a few influences (or seeds) to analyze and see if what you are doing is in alignment with your vision or the "garden" you wish to produce. In other words, the influences in your daily life can be but are not necessarily all bad things. You must be willing to ask yourself frequently about what habits may be "good seeds or bad seeds." However, it will also be important to assess which ones are pushing you towards your destiny and which are just time stealers or inhibitors of healthy growth in the garden of your heart and mind.

Entertainment
Movies, media, video games, television

Reading Material
Magazines, newspapers, books, articles, social media

People
Friends, family, class-mates, co-workers, etc. (albeit, you cannot always control some of these influences, you can limit the time you spend with them or work on being an influencer instead of being influenced)

Music
Paying close attention to the messages they are sending

Social Media
Limiting time spent unless it aligns with your vision and monitoring what you allow yourself to be exposed to

Education or Insights
YouTube, audiobooks, courses, training or seminars. Are they pushing you toward your destiny?

When it comes to taking care of our garden to ensure it matches our vision and pushes us toward our desired goals, we must do whatever is necessary to change our inner dialogue.

Therefore, a regular examination of our influences, both inner and outer will not only reveal some root causes of stress in our lives but it can help us prioritize what we allow ourselves to become involved in and help us to regain control in all areas. This is something we should be doing periodically, especially if we are noticing some "hiccups" in our progress.

FOURTH ASSIGNMENT:

Take a brief inventory of seven inner and outer influences. Write them down based on the following areas:

OUTER:

- ✓ The people you spend most of your time with
- ✓ The types of games, media or entertainment you indulge in
- ✓ Books or articles you are investing your time and thoughts into
- ✓ Studies or lack of studies in areas you desire to grow in
- ✓ The amount of time you spend on social media
- ✓ The type of activities you are choosing to be involved in
- ✓ The level of fitness you are committed to

INNER:

- ✓ The ratio of positive vs. negative thoughts of the 60,000 you have per day
- ✓ The value of new concepts you spend time thinking about
- ✓ The amount of time you spend creating lists and utilizing your will power to stay on track
- ✓ Visualizing consistently
- ✓ Time spent working on goals or dreams

✓ Regular time frames to unplug, spending down time to relax internally

✓ Time spent processing your mind sets with objectivity, maintaining a willingness to change them

Once you have written down your inner and outer influences, evaluate what changes you need to make and create a brief list of what you will work on. It should only take 20-30 minutes to complete this exercise. The difference it will make can save you hours of grief, fog, confusion, frustration, regrets and energy loss.

> **SUCCESS ROUTINE TIP #4:**
>
> When we can feel and see the improvements and changes as we remain daily cognizant of our thinking habits, we can create consistent progress. This progress becomes evident very quickly and can produce a harvest, which inspires us to keep the weeds out and continue to sow the right seeds. The momentum we create in developing the right thinking habits is what will push us forward faster than we may expect.

This quote is a powerful principle in the analysis of the Garden:

"Progress equals Happiness."

– Tony Robbins

ROUTINE BUILDERS FROM CHAPTER FOUR

1. If you did the assignment in this chapter, you should have created a list of habits and behaviors that must change. Look at that list and develop a plan of action on how you might maintain and nurture your garden every day going forward:

_____

_____

_____

_____

_____

_____

_____

_____

_____

_____

_____

_____

_____

_____

_____

_____

_____

CHAPTER FIVE –
HEART SCIENCE,
ENERGY AND THE
LAW OF
ATTRACTION

In the last chapter, we mentioned that your heart has 40,000 specialized neuron-like cells called cardiac intrinsic ganglia or little brain of the heart.[6]

Each section of ganglia functions like neurons but have a very special assignment that is distinctly different from the 100 billion neurons in your brain. Both your brain and your heart are producing electromagnetic energy at a rate of approximately 400 billion actions per second. This energy is necessary for sustaining life, as well as, possessing creative ability. See Figure X (below) for locations of ganglia found in cadaver hearts.

Figure X

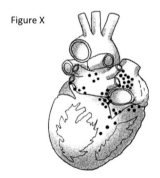

According to the Director of Research of the HeartMath Institute, Rollin McCraty, a recognized global leader in emotional physiology, optimal function, resilience and stress-management research, "The heart generates the largest electromagnetic field in the body. The electrical field as measured in an electrocardiogram (ECG) is about 60 times greater in amplitude than the brain waves recorded in an electroencephalogram (EEG)."[7] This energy or field

---

[6] https://www.sciencedirect.com/science/article/pii/S0022522396700946)
[7] https://www.heartmath.org/articles-of-the-heart/science-of-the-heart/the-energetic-heart-is-unfolding/

is measured in magnetometers, several feet away with a Superconducting Quantum Interference Device (SQUID).

In fact, the magnetometers are gauged by emotion. Such measurements were taken in an experiment at the HeartMath Institute where tests were performed by provoking specific emotions within test subjects. The findings were eye opening in regards to the importance of our state of mind and our ability to master emotional intelligence.

During these tests, when subjects produced emotions such as love, joy, compassion and gratitude, the level of magnetometers were roughly 500-600 in range. When subjects produced emotions such as agreement, cooperation and problem solving, the level of magnetometers were roughly 200-350 in range. In addition, when subjects produced emotions such as hate, envy, bitterness and offense, the level of magnetometers were roughly 20-100 in range. So, why is this important to understand in regards to building a success routine? The answer is quite simple. In fact, we don't necessarily need the statistics from the research mentioned above to figure it all out:

Others can sense how you feel about another person or situation at any given moment in time without you even saying a word. The energy your heart produces is unmistakable. Think about the last time you were with your significant other or perhaps a relative or friend who was angry with you for some reason. Or you may have walked into a room where the tension was high or people were arguing. You could sense the bad energy in the room, even if they responded with a fake smile and said, "Everything is just fine."

You have the same ability as a dog to sense fear. The big difference between you and the dog is that humans are not always "in tune" with this energy. Yet, we use it every day, subconsciously, to decipher our interpretation of others in their reactions to us or their attitudes toward us.

This energy is real. It can even be the determining factor on whether you win over an employer in a job interview or make a sale in a business deal. Body language, facial expressions and vocal tones are important, too. All of us know a "fake" when we meet one. They may have the right stance, posture, body language and vocal tones but if in their hearts they are not authentic, we can pick up on it immediately.

Pure common sense tells us that when we can master our emotional response to all of what life brings to us, we can literally choose an energy that will either attract or repel. In light of this information, ask yourself these questions:

1. If I choose to produce and maintain emotions such as love, joy, peace, patience, kindness, goodness, faithfulness, forgiveness, gentleness and self-control, practicing gratitude and compassion, will it open new doors of opportunity for me in life and career?

2. If I choose to produce and maintain emotions such as hatred, offense, insecurity, jealousy, bitterness, doubt, rage, anger, anxiety and a critical, judgmental mindset, will it close doors of opportunity for me in life and career?

CASE STUDY #5

TAMMY'S STORY

Being a single mom is challenging enough in today's world but for Tammy, it was a bit overwhelming. She couldn't seem to figure out how to keep up with her full-time job, take care of housework, shop for groceries, meet the daily needs of her family and be the mom she really wanted to be. Having gone through a tumultuous time with her ex-husband, she wasn't even sure about who she was supposed to be, no less trying to meet the needs of others.

For the sake of finding some sort of peace in her disrupted life, she struggled through every day trying to please the people and be the person everyone else wanted her to be. She knew this was not what she wanted, but in reality, she didn't really know what to do with her future or how to make it happen.

For Tammy, living became more like survival. The idea of fulfillment seemed impossible.

Tammy had only a few people she could talk to about her hardships and one of them was her co-worker, Robert. Robert always seemed so positive and would often try to encourage her. In fact, she was amazed at his relentless pursuit to reach his goals. Robert was on a journey to become the person he knew he wanted to be and this inspired Tammy.

Eventually, Robert introduced Tammy and I, opening the door to her new journey.

First, Tammy developed her new personal vision statement and selected goals that would push her toward her destiny. Each day, as she incorporated a new way of living by adopting her new success routine, she found herself visualizing a different future. A future filled with new ambitions, new hope and a whole new lifestyle.

The first thing she wanted to overcome was her morning routine. Up until now, she and her son had extreme difficulties getting up early enough. Tardiness for her son was far too frequent. Additionally, the stress levels Tammy was experiencing was having an effect on her son's performance at school.

With the new success routine in place, things really began to change for them both. She was rising early enough to actually enjoy her son and have time to prepare her mind and body for the day ahead without feeling rushed.

Tammy became more focused and driven in pursuing her dreams. The more she poured herself into this pursuit, the more things began to happen for her. People she never met before became keys in assisting her with some portion of her vision. Opportunities began to just appear in front of her, building so much excitement and hope about her future and her aspirations.

At times, Tammy could barely contain herself with excitement and zeal. She lived in expectation for what might happen every day. The more excited she became, the easier it was to get up earlier and the more things continued to fall into her path.

The new, daily concepts of goal setting and pursuing a sound state of mind became a sworn life style change for her. Through the changes occurring in Tammy, her son also began setting goals and living with different perceptions causing his grades and his demeanor to improve.

After five weeks, Tammy made the investment to continue with the program and success routine. In the days following, she was able to completely, overcome the confusion, hurt and frustration from her former relationship and even created a mutual agreement with her ex-husband. The agreement ended the unrest and opened doors to a more cohesive interchange between them.

Tammy turned around almost every difficult situation in her world and was excited about moving forward in her life. She also found out that when you change your perceptions and keep your focus on what you desire, good things will always come your way.

COGNITIVE DISSONANCE AND COGNITIVE CONSONANCE

We touched on Cognitive Dissonance and Consonance in Chapter Three, while discussing the power of affirmations. However, it is important that you grasp the science behind these terms and understand why you must make it your goal to create complete synchronicity between your heart and mind.

Since the heart and the brain both have neurons or neuron-like cells and electromagnetic activity, they are always communicating with each other. In fact, the connection between the two is vital to human emotion, as well as, accomplishment in life and career.

Leon Festinger was the first developer of the Cognitive Dissonance Theory in 1957. This theory states that dissonance stems from unpleasant feelings of discomfort that result from holding two conflicting beliefs internally. I like to describe it as *when your heart is not in agreement with your head*. The opposing term for this is Cognitive Consonance or in my definition, *when your heart and your head are in complete agreement.*

To help you understand the role this plays in our ability to influence others and ourselves, let's put it parenthetically: A man desires to be a leader so he signs up for multiple courses on leadership. He aces every course and is hired in to an executive position based on his impressive credentials. In fact, he appears to understand leadership even better than most of his peers and some of his superiors. However, in his heart, he lacks confidence due to deeply rooted neural networks that cause him to frequently, question his abilities. Despite the knowledge of leadership he may have in his mind, he struggles daily with self-doubt, often tending to "people pleasing" instead of leading. Furthermore, there is a sense of awkwardness and a lack of authenticity in his communications with his team. As the team picks up on this, and they will, they instinctively lose trust in him and will eventually lose respect for him. He may experience moments or even days when his knowledge is enough to give him the confidence he needs to lead. However, the insecurities that lurk in his heart will frequently overpower the knowledge he has in his mind, stealing away his ability to maintain a strong presence of leadership.

This scenario plays out in multiple lives every day, at many different levels. Cognitive dissonance adversely affects relationships, success, sales and a multitude of other life and career challenges.

Until cognitive consonance can be achieved, an internal struggle will remain constant and relentless. In some cases, it can be absolutely maddening.

So how do we achieve cognitive consonance with our hearts and minds? This entire book from beginning to end is dedicated to helping you develop a daily routine that will empower you to build a new way of thinking and perceiving. Ultimately, creating a solid success routine, this in time can create cognitive consonance in areas of belief that held you back for years. Areas where you lacked confidence or felt "stuck" or somewhat "cursed" because Mom, Dad, or Great Grandpa told you that is what or who you are.

It is even possible that something traumatic or hurtful happened to you and you processed the whole experience in the worst way. Through the natural inclination of human behavior, your subconscious went into a defense or survival mode. During this time, you may have convinced yourself of something that is entirely untrue about your abilities, talents or intelligence. If a success routine is not put into place and adhered to, long term, changes cannot occur. Hence, cognitive dissonance is allowed to continue.

At this point in the book, you should be contemplating the changes you must make if you want to achieve your full potential and rise to greatness.

However, be warned that although the decision to move forward is the biggest step, it is only the beginning. No matter who we are or what our current state of mind may be, we will always encounter "walls" or barriers that can inhibit our progress, such as:

- ✓ The atmosphere and culture we live in

- ✓ The fears that attempt to take us over and stifle our faith or belief in who we are called to become

- ✓ The old patterns in daily routine that pull us back to what is comfortable, prohibiting us from a new routine that can change our world

- ✓ The temptation to put other things ahead of our daily "training" with a mindset that our growth is not a priority

- ✓ A mindset of denial, believing that we cannot experience total transformation if we will put forth a daily effort

✓ The lack of practice in using our mental faculties we are gifted with by our creator

✓ The strongholds that are placed in our minds by poor mindsets which need to be broken through replacement

FIFTH ASSIGNMENT:

In order to create powerful heart energy in every area of our lives and develop Cognitive Consonance, we must raise up new standards to live by and set up a solid action plan for the changes we must make in our routine.

Below is a brief list of standards you can assess to develop a plan of attack! For each item on the list, consider what you must do to alter your heart energy and focus. Then decide what new habits you will have to adopt in your daily routine to accomplish these changes.

☐ Health & Fitness

☐ Career Advancement

☐ State of Mind or Daily Motivation

☐ Goal Setting

☐ Relationships

☐ Sowing Into the Lives of Others

SUCCESS ROUTINE TIP #5:

Time Out for YOU! Managing "Heart Energy" and achieving Cognitive Consonance is not a "once and done" process but a life-long commitment. It is a lifestyle. The only way to maintain the right heart energy is to be intentional about every moment of every day.

ROUTINE BUILDERS FROM CHAPTER FIVE

1. Think about the opportunities, connections, promotions or positions you desire to reach within the 1-5 years. List them below:

_____

_____

_____

_____

_____

_____

_____

2. Based on the information in this chapter, what will you have to change in your life and your daily routine in order to see these doors open for you? List what changes you will have to make and how you will make them:

_____

_____

_____

_____

_____

_____

_____

_____

CHAPTER SIX –
THE BIGGEST
KILLER OF ENERGY,
PASSION AND
DREAMS

You can apply all you have learned throughout this book but you can be stopped right in your tracks from making progress if you have **Un-forgiveness** in your heart. This may seem like a peculiar subject for a book on "Greatness". However, it could be the most important step in your journey. In fact, if you have struggled in the past with overcoming certain obstacles in your life or felt frustrated that you cannot make progress; this chapter could change everything for you!

First, let me make something clear: Forgiving a suffered wrong does not mean that you forget or that the offender is absolved of the offense. Wrong is wrong and the pain you may have suffered is real. Additionally, the choice is yours in the end. I hope you will take the time to read this chapter all the way through before making any decisions. Choosing to forgive is more about releasing you, than it is about releasing them.

Ask yourself a few questions and try to stay objective with your responses:

By choosing not to forgive . . .

- ✓ Are you suffering emotionally, mentally or physically?

- ✓ Are you resolving this issue and making life better or bitter?

- ✓ Is it possible that you are damaging your relationships around you due to anxiety?

- ✓ Could you be missing out on opportunities in life or career due to your state of mind and/or health conditions brought on by the un-forgiveness?

✓ Could you be creating neural networks that are eschewing your perceptions on marriage, family, jobs, politics, religion, social interaction, investments, education, confidence and other areas?

✓ Finally, do you feel the offender could be lying awake at night unable to sleep and feeling tormented because you don't forgive them? (Not likely)

Let's dive into just a few real consequences of choosing not to forgive, beginning with your mental and physical health[8]:

SIX EMOTIONAL EFFECTS OF BITTERNESS (UN-FORGIVENESS)

1. Prolonged mental and Emotional pain

2. Anxiety and/or Depression

3. Vindictive behaviors

4. Distrust

5. Cynicism and Pessimism

6. Futility & Unhappiness

---

[8] Psychology Today. https://www.psychologytoday.com/blog/evolution-the-self/201501/don-t-let-your-anger-mature-bitterness

SIX PHYSICAL EFFECTS OF BITTERNESS (UN-FORGIVENESS)

1. Insomnia

2. Hypertension

3. Back pain

4. Headaches

5. Abdominal conditions

6. Unhealthy immune system

In 2010, Dr. Michael Barry wrote in his book, The Forgiveness Project, that 61% of cancer patients have forgiveness issues and of those, more than half are severe. He also stated, "Harboring these negative emotions, this anger and hatred, creates a state of chronic anxiety."

> *"Refusing to forgive makes people sick and keeps them that way."*
>
> *– Dr. Steven Standiford, Chief of Surgery*
> *Cancer Treatment Centers of America*

CASE STUDY #6

DEBORAH'S STORY

Anxiety and depression were not strangers to Deborah. She had struggled with very serious issues for over a decade. Like so many of us, early in life, she came face to face with many situations and circumstances she simply did not know how to deal with. With each challenge, she gave it her best and then tried to make sense of it, often overthinking each issue. Deborah was and still is a person who carries a strong desire to be excellent in every way. In fact, she developed a habit of trying too hard to make things right or make others happy. Eventually, it ended up driving her to a place of deep dissatisfaction, not only in the outcomes of each challenge but even within herself.

In her attempts to gain some kind of relief, she tried a multitude of treatments, counselors and therapists. All of her attempts to resolve her issues availed very little, if any, results. At times, hopelessness tried to take over her.

Deborah had a decent career, a fine husband who loved her and children she cherished. However, the black cloud that was over her life was constant and unbearable. It had been so long since she felt "normal" about her problems that she had forgotten what it was like.

Furthermore, the fact that things were "not really as bad as they seemed" only made her feel worse about her depression because she couldn't shake off the disappointment she had in herself. It could even be said that she was unable to forgive herself for the way she was processing life. This downward spiral had been out of control for so long that Deborah had completely lost her way back.

The company where she worked was holding their annual, all staff training day and I was the lunch keynote. The topic was Communicating with Resilience Under Pressure. For the first time in her life, Deborah had the opportunity to learn the science behind thoughts and how stress can alter our physiology. She became very intrigued with this possibility so she followed up after the training.

Our first discussion revealed her brokenness and desire to break free from the grip of the crippling effects of depression. However, she was very reluctant since nothing had worked for her in the past.

After some time passed, she realized she needed to try something different, so she took the leap and began her new journey.

She wrote out her personal vision statement and determined which goals would be most helpful to her, personally and professionally.

For five weeks straight, she filled her mind with powerful and insightful teachings through podcasts, audiobooks, quotes, articles, gratitude lists and much more, being sure to write down her thoughts and track her progress.

Deborah was learning to be consumed daily with positive, forward thinking and intentional information pushing her into her vision. With each passing day, it got easier and more fluent. She also worked on adopting very important habits to assist her in a complete routine makeover. She was exercising as often as she could, even if only for 15 or 20 minutes at time. She was visualizing and she was taking time out for herself and her family. In addition, she was becoming increasingly cognizant of empowering other people in her world, spreading joy and kindness. The more Deborah stepped out of her past and into her future, the more hope arose. After about 3 weeks, she was noticing dramatic changes in her physiology. She found herself smiling more, celebrating the small things more and enjoying life. She was finding new energy and was excited about where this was taking her.

After six weeks, Deborah made so much progress that it had become evident to her supervisor, her family members and all those who were close to her. So much so, they called to thank me and offer to buy more coaching so she could continue her journey out of darkness.

"Thank you for giving me my daughter back,"

—Deborah's Mom

Please note: Having a success routine is not an absolute cure for all cases of depression; however, our thoughts are very powerful in the composition of chemical balance for both body and mind. Deborah will have to keep up her success routine long term, if she is to recover completely. She did not get in her condition overnight and she will not reverse all of it overnight. However, she now has a chance and the tools she needs to continue her journey to recovery.

"Thoughts are real, physical things that occupy mental real estate. Moment by moment, every day, you are changing the structure of your brain through your thinking. When we hope, it is an activity of the mind that changes the structure of our brain in a positive and normal direction."

—Caroline Leaf, Cognitive Neuroscientist
Best-selling author of Switch on Your Brain

THE 4-STEP JOURNEY TO FORGIVENESS

Forgiveness is rarely an event but a process or journey. As stated at the beginning of this chapter, the pain we can feel from betrayal, suffering or loss is very real and can take time to work through. Forgiving a wrong does not mean we are declaring that what happened to us is okay. Nor does is require you to pretend you don't remember the offense. And in some cases, those who have brought the offense are no longer with us or we are unable to communicate with them directly. Regardless of your current relationship with the offender, the choice to forgive is extremely important for YOU!

There are multiple benefits when we choose to work through the process and forgive. Here are just a few:

- As long as we allow the offense to hold us in un-forgiveness, we are shackled to that offender and ultimately, to our past. Forgiving sets us free from those chains so we can, once again, find freedom in ourselves.

- When we forgive, in time, we alter our body chemistry or physiology, both in our bodies and minds, increasing our energy, calming our senses and restoring our health.

- We rediscover our lives and slowly our happiness returns and our state of mind improves.

Follow these steps below and work through them every day for as long as it takes:

STEP #1: IDENTIFY THE HURT OR OFFENSE

Label the offense and label the feelings you may have as a result. Be as specific as you can. Consider writing them down on a sheet of paper and then destroying it or burying it as a way of symbolically declaring an "end" to your suffering.

- ✓ Who or what caused this offense?

- ✓ What was the offense?

- ✓ How did you feel at the time?

- ✓ How do you feel now?

STEP #2: CONFESS ANY HATRED YOU MAY HAVE

It is not wrong to hate what may have happened or caused your offense. However, it is what you do about the hate, which will determine the outcome. Here are some considerations:

- Projecting the hatred inwards, stuffing it down or harboring the grudge will wreak havoc in our health, our minds and our ability to function; ultimately leading to disease, depression and multiple other issues.

- Projecting the hatred outwardly will likely destroy our healthy relationships and wreak damage to our world around us including our personal and professional performance. Taking out hatred on the offender will never solve the issue. It will only increase our frustration and potentially bring harm to our future.

- Deciding to hate **the offense itself** rather than the offender (the "sin instead of the sinner") is the healthiest direction to take in the first stages of forgiveness. Simply make the shift in your heart and mind that you will despise the offense and release the offender.

STEP #3: ACKNOWLEDGE AND RELINQUISH CONTROL

Refusing to forgive provides a feeling of control or power over the offender but the reality is that we cannot control others. In many cases, the offender is unaffected by our decision to hold them captive by our un-forgiveness. The feelings of control we have are only a mask burying our true feelings. Make the following declarations every day:

- ✓ I refuse to be a victim!

- ✓ I choose to cancel a debt I cannot collect

- ✓ I make the decision to be free and move forward

- ✓ I allow God, Karma, the Universe to be my vindicator and bring justice

- ✓ I sever any ties and relinquish all control between myself and the offender

STEP #4: BEGIN TO ALLOW HEALING AND RESTORATION IN YOUR HEART AND MIND

Day by day, make the above declarations and begin to choose a path of healing, allowing your heart and mind to be filled with warm thoughts of love and compassion for yourself.

Take time to pamper and love on yourself with walks in the park, long baths or anything that gives you a sense of wholeness and well-being. Each time, meditate on your wholeness and happiness.

Use the following affirmations over yourself to aid in this stage of forgiveness:

- ✓ I am calm, secure and hopeful

- ✓ I am filled with joy and strength

- ✓ I am an overcomer in all things

- ✓ I am blessed and valuable

- ✓ I am talented and highly favored

- ✓ I live each day with anticipation for a new life

Allow yourself time and feel free to express any emotions you need to as you work through this process. Cry, shout, vent and share with someone you trust. Even in moments of solitude, this can be very therapeutic. Prayers, journaling and meditation are also very effective in helping you to sort out your feelings and detach yourself from the offense. As long as your goal is to reach the other side.

There is a Step #5 if you would like to take this to an even higher level. If possible, consider writing a letter forgiving the offender and sending it to them or telling them you forgive them. You can also pray for them, speak blessings over them or give them a gift of peace. This action is a bold step that can bring incredible restoration and a sense of completeness. Additionally, if you believe in reaping and sowing or karma, this action can change your destiny for amazing, new opportunities.

As you apply each step and time passes, the offense will diminish and your freedom from it will become evident, resulting in a magnificent future far above the place you once stood and opening new doors for you.

SIXTH ASSIGNMENT:

1. Consider anyone in your life, past or present, whom you may be holding a grudge. It could even be yourself. Write their names below:

   1. _____
   2. _____
   3. _____
   4. _____
   5. _____

SUCCESS ROUTINE TIP #6:

Taking revenge or holding a grudge is like pouring a glass of poison for the offender and drinking it yourself.

ROUTINE BUILDERS FROM CHAPTER SIX

1. Forgiving a wrong does not mean we are declaring that what happened to us is okay. Nor does is require you to pretend you don't remember the offense.

   Now, beginning with each name, work through the 4 Steps to Forgiveness exercise in this chapter. Take as much time as you need with each name but determine to stick with it until you forgive every name on your list.

GREATNESS TIP 6: Assignment #6 about forgiveness could be one of the hardest things you have ever done but the freedom you will have when you complete this portion of the journey will thrust you forward as if a dam has broken and the water that has been held back for so long is finally free to flow.

CHAPTER SEVEN – GETTING "UNSTUCK" IN YOUR MIND AND HEART

In the last chapter we covered forgiveness of an offense. Hopefully, you have chosen to release this portion of your heart that is being restrained from moving forward so that you can take one more step into your destiny.

Be aware that there is another very important part of forgiveness that could also be holding your heart captive. It is stomping on every effort you have or will make to raise your standards. This part may even be more difficult than the last step. It is letting go of the past.

For each of us, there are times in our lives or careers where we have developed a deep sense of regret, remorse or anger toward ourselves. Sometimes, it is something we feel we "allowed" to happen to us, even if we were ignorant or helpless at the time. It could be partially our fault or it could be something we had no control over. Other times it may be something we tried to "fix" or "save" but for whatever reason, we failed and lost something or someone valuable. Whatever the case may be, choosing to live in the past or dwell on a loss is the worst kind of unforgiveness; an unforgiveness toward ourselves. Remaining in this state chains us to our past and traps us from moving forward.

In Chapter Two, you learned about the importance of having a VISION and your assignment was writing your own personal Vision Statement. This step was intended to help you focus forward rather than backward. Yet, if you do not deal with whatever regrets or remorse you may have inwardly about something in your past, you will be in Cognitive Dissonance. When you are in dissonance, every affirmation, new thought or action becomes null and void. Just as your Vision Statement can become real in your mind and heart bringing it toward you, rehearsing or recalling negative experiences send you in the opposite direction.

In other words, each time you react according to past experiences rather than adhering to your new thought life and vision for the future, you send electrical impulses into old neural pathways strengthening their connectivity. This habit sustains old mindsets allowing them to remain dominant since they have deeper and wider connections than the new ones.

Here are seven questions to ask yourself about your past and potentially destructive thinking patterns:

- ☐ Were you told by someone you trusted, admired or depended upon that you were "no good" or "stupid," or perhaps something similar?

- ☐ Did you ever struggle with a subject, relationship or job where you failed time and time again, making you feel like a failure in that area and convincing you that you were just "not good at it"?

- ☐ Have you ever tried to succeed at something you were passionate about but the circumstances, at the time, prevented you from succeeding and convinced you that it just wasn't a good idea for you to try again?

- ☐ Did you experience a broken trust in your life or career when someone seriously let you down, hurt you or devastated you, making you feel that you could never trust again in that way?

- ☐ Was there ever an occasion where you tried very hard to impress and no matter what you did, it was never enough?

Thus, causing you to decide in your heart that the pain of rejection you felt made it not worth trying again.

☐ Did you have something catastrophic happen to you in your life or career that made you feel hopeless, lost or uncertain about you, your future and/or your abilities?

☐ Have you ever lost someone or something in your life or career which made you feel it was your fault and you have been blaming yourself ever since that time?

SEVENTH ASSIGNMENT

Check the box for each of the seven questions which pertain to you personally, pull yourself out of your own skin (disconnect from all emotions) and objectively think about whether your beliefs could be true.

If you find yourself feeling "stuck", again and again, in forming long lasting relationships, solid business plans, successful endeavors or just feeling good about you, then read on...this chapter is for YOU!

Below are four lies we buy into, forming mindsets, which keep us "stuck" and unable to move forward into our greatness:

LIES WE BELIEVE ABOUT OURSELVES:

Perhaps, you have bought into a lie you were told or believed about yourself from someone you looked up to. If we are truly honest about it and are willing to work at altering our perceptions through cognitive transformation methods, we may discover that the lies we have accepted as truth for so long can no longer control us.

"Other people's opinion of you does not have to become your reality."

— Les Brown

WALLS WE BUILD AROUND OURSELVES:

Hurts, disappointments and rejection are all very real and very painful. Unknowingly, we build up walls around ourselves to prevent these things from ever happening again. To some degree, we could justify it as being wise or cautious. But, for many, the incident is over-inflated from rehearsing it to the point that it has completely shut us down to an unhealthy degree. Ultimately, we have built up a strong neural network that is affecting us in all of our relationships. Through a commitment of brain training, over time, we can restore our mindsets, raising our emotional and social intelligence.

INNER VOWS:

When we encounter situations, events or circumstances where we find ourselves backed against the wall or strongly opposed to whatever is happening, we can unknowingly create "Inner Vows". I knew someone who made an inner vow concerning soda pop. He grew up restricted from drinking any soda pop by his parents. The day he moved out as an adult, he filled his closet with soda pop and became almost "pushy" about offering it to any guest who visited his apartment. Additionally, he drank it with every meal despite its unhealthy consequences. There are many other examples I could use but I hope this one helps you to see where you may have made your own "inner vows".

FEAR OF FAILURE:

Inevitably, all of us will fail throughout our lives. This is not a news flash for any of us. However, there are times when a failure can trap us, destroying our potential and discouraging us from pushing through into success. In fact, when a failure is perceived wrongly, it ends up acting more like a rejection causing us to rehearse it over and over. Instead of being the foundation for growth and learning, we ultimately allow it to become a stumbling block that trips us up and damages us for life. No matter how big the failure, when we determine in our minds that we are unable or ill equipped, we sell ourselves short and stunt our opportunity for advancement in life and career.

Despite your setbacks, you have what it takes for GREATNESS! You CAN create a new you, a new destiny and open the doors to new opportunities. Give yourself permission to forgive anything in your past that may have created success inhibiting, mind blocks. Decide to let the past be the past. You must do this in order to achieve a fixed and solid focus on your future. Only then can you establish a mindset that will make your affirmations more powerful and create cognitive consonance. You will experience a clear, peaceful and stable state of mind that will propel you into amazing realities you never thought possible. This freedom is required if you want to continue on Your Journey to GREATNESS Through Routine.

Listed are several names you may recognize as those who did not allow damaging remarks, failures, struggles or deceptions from their past get in the way of winning:[9]

Thomas Edison was told he was "too stupid to learn" by his teacher and fired by his first employers for being "unproductive". He even failed 1,000 times at perfecting the lightbulb. Still his determined spirit responded, *"I didn't fail 1,000 times, the light bulb was an invention with 1,000 steps."*

Henry Ford failed and went broke five times before he succeeded at inventing the Ford motor car.

Michael Jordan stated, "I've missed more than 9000 shots in my career. I've lost almost 300 games; 26 times, I've been trusted to take the game winning shot ... and missed. I've failed over and over and over again in my life. That is why I succeed."

Walt Disney was fired, bankrupted and rejected. A newspaper editor said, "He lacked imagination and had no good ideas." The city of Anaheim told him he'd only attract lowlifes to the amusement park the world now knows as Disneyland.

Lucille Ball began studying to be an actress in 1927. The head instructor of the John Murray Anderson Drama School told her to "try any other profession," but those words did not stop her.

Colonel Sanders was a man who started at 65 and failed 1009 times before succeeding. Whether you like KFC or not, the story of Colonel Harland Sanders is truly amazing. He has become a

---

[9] https://www.uky.edu/~eushe2/Pajares/OnFailingG.html

renowned figure by marketing his "finger lickin' good", Kentucky Fried Chicken. [10]

---

[10] https://yourstory.com/search?q=colonel+sanders

CASE STUDY #7

SOPHIA'S STORY

This story is unique as it begins with a list of setbacks and unfortunate circumstances, personally and professionally. However, due to the application of many practices shared in this book, Sophia created a dynamic success routine for herself that ultimately turned many things around for her at multiple levels.

The story begins after a 4-year streak of life-altering challenges for Sophia and her family including:

✓ *Job loss from company downsizing*

✓ *Serious injury leaving her unable to walk for 9 months and unable to drive for many of those months*

✓ *A failed business venture*

✓ *Another job loss from a business closing*

✓ *Yes, one more job loss from a company closing its United States office*

✓ *A house with ongoing structural issues, despite repairs and complete replacement of multiple areas*

✓ *House flooding which destroyed the main level and insurance didn't cover ground water flooding*

✓ *Husband's unexpected, life-threatening health issue and an injury resulting in complete loss of income for more than 12 months. That was in addition to her own income loss*

✓ *A plethora of uninsured medical expenses*

✓ *Eventual home foreclosure*

All of the above happened immediately after the loss of her financial resources, when a dishonest investment company dissolved their business, shortly after taking all of their savings and investment funds.

To top it off, her favorite dog died. Sophia's life was like a bad country song!

In the midst of all of this, she fought hard to keep her head above water. She willingly worked every job, even those that she never imagined she would settle for. Her earnings were a fraction of the pay rate she previously earned. She was downtrodden, guilt-ridden and exasperated by all of the failures and the difficult circumstances that continued to occur. Despite her present efforts or prior achievements, all seemed hopeless. Nevertheless, amidst the chaos, Sophia was determined not to give up. It was at this time she reached out to me.

Soon after, she began a daily routine of encouragement, including motivational videos for morning inspiration and audio books for personal development. She also worked hard on a daily affirmation program. Her pursuits for knowledge and changes in her mindsets included in-depth research of many helpful topics that fascinated and empowered her. Topics such as:

- Effective personal affirmations

- Visualization techniques

- Epigenetics

- Neuroscience

- Quantum physics

121

Being of Christian faith, she was especially intrigued about the way all the topics she was studying aligned with instructions given in the Bible for life, success and happiness.

Sophia continued on this new path of learning while continuing to grow and retrain her brain. She was very excited about her vision of complete restoration. She believed she would see far more than she lost. She even wrote down a list of specific things she wanted to see and continued to work on believing, speaking and pursuing. Her focus and conversation diverted from complaining and worrying about things she could not control to talking about things she believed in her heart would truly happen.

A new home was one of the things high on her list. After she wrote down every detail of what she wanted in a home, she began searching for something that fit that description. Sophia diligently spent every moment she could afford looking at many homes. Keep in mind that she had no money, no credit and no equity in the home that she was losing and had limited time with the bank to get out.

The second thing on her "critical needs" list was a job. She had become very good at job-hunting but this time she came at it with strong a belief in obtaining the right job. Interestingly, a position materialized for her. During introductions in her first week at work, she discovered that this employer shared many of her same Christian values. When her co-workers asked if they could pray for her, one of them shared that Sophia was praying for a home closer to work. As the prayers and conversations continued, another co-worker spoke up and asked, "You don't happen to want a lake house, do you?"

This was a shock to her because a lake house was exactly what she had written on her list and had been visualizing. Upon receiving more details, she discovered it could be a "rent to own" opportunity. This could not have been a better set up for her, especially considering her financial circumstances. All of this happened just within the time frame she needed to in order to meet the deadline on the foreclosure.

Below is the exact list of affirmations Sophia wrote and sent to me, detailing the home she was visualizing. It includes her check marks and notes describing the fulfillment of each one on the list:

✓ *I'm going to have a house on a lake - on one of the top two lakes I'd been searching!*

✓ *I'd like it to have just two bedrooms so it's less work to maintain – got it!*

✓ *I don't want a lot of stairs to get into the house - it had a ramp!*

✓ *I really want the laundry on the main level – got it!*

✓ *Even though I only need 2 bedrooms, I still want a 2nd bathroom - it has 2 full bathrooms!*

✓ *I want the yard to have a gradual decline from the house to the water, so it's not uncomfortably steep to walk down, but also not in danger of flooding - perfectly gradual!*

✓ *It has to have a sandy-bottom waterfront, where I can walk in gradually without slime or swampy muck or weed - pristine sand!*

✓ *It has to have a lot of large windows overlooking the water - the entire waterfront is a wall of floor-to-ceiling windows!*

✓ *The lake has to be deep enough to have the right kind of fish that my husband likes to fish for - perch and walleye included!*

✓ *It has to be an all-sports lake so we can boat, once we get a boat – got it!*

✓ *It still needs to be relatively peaceful on the water and with generous distance in proximity to neighbors - it's on a dead-end road and the neighbors are seasonal. They are rarely there!*

✓ *I joked that I didn't care if the house had ugly wallpaper – well, let's just say, it's not my style.*

✓ *I also said I didn't even care if the lake house had an ugly kitchen (I was a bit sad about giving up the new kitchen we'd purchased and had installed in the old house) - the kitchen was so ugly! Ha-ha! ...with lots of great storage though!*

Amazingly, the lake property was worth more than double the value of the home Sophia lost. She was very thankful and excited for what was next in her life. In her own words, she stated, "It has only just begun!"

The following are words she wrote as a testimonial offering for this book:

"Michelle dragged me out of my hopelessness when I had become too exhausted of my circumstances to push forward on my own. She reached out with her hand of inspiration to lift me up and push me forward, motivating me into the truth of my

purpose. She was the only one. Everyone else tried to limit me within my circumstances. More than ever, I was tempted to limit myself. I am so grateful for the tools she shared with me. These intentional practices truly change everything."

"Don't worry about failures, worry about the chances you miss when you don't even try."

—Jack Canfield, Chicken Soup for the Soul

As crazy as it sounds, one of the things I had to learn years ago was to expect trials and adversities rather than trying to dodge them. Not that I focused ON them or visualized them because that would be counterproductive and it would contradict everything I have been sharing in this book. Instead, I came to the realization that tough times, failures and challenges are unavoidable. Living a life hoping they won't happen is a false pretense and will always catch us unprepared. When we live with this mindset, we set ourselves up to be overtaken by life's challenges. It takes us to a point where we develop habits of reactive thinking. This type of thinking then sets off a downward spiral of disappointment, hurt, anger and a victim's mentality. This reactive response will inevitably lead us into depression, disease and both, mental and physical illness. Think about the word, "Dis-ease". Although the common definition means illness, the origin of the word is French, meaning "lack of ease". This can then be correlated with many of the things we have already discussed like cognitive dissonance, unforgiveness, lack of confidence, offense and multiples of others.

Allowing the habit of reactivity into our lives and careers, places us right back into old mindsets and sets us up for disaster on every front. By choosing to react negatively, we are sending our electrical impulses firing off through past neural networks. The unfortunate fact is that these past networks may be on the brink of becoming obsolete in areas where we are working on retraining our brain. In doing so, we revive old habits by breathing new life into them and ultimately, resurrecting them. On each occasion where we succumb to these old patterns, the neurosynaptic response automatically triggers a release of toxic hormones all over again and we re-establish old routines, leading us right back to disease, depression, etc. The only way to avoid this vicious cycle is to maintain a consistent "success routine".

Just as in the story of Sophia, resolve to rise up every day and make a choice to bolster your mind and heart by filling it with the right information. Empower yourself with thoughts and feelings that will equip you to stand strong against anything that may distract or discourage you. Yet at the same time, maintain the mindset of expectation for good things to happen and get serious about your destiny!

> **SUCCESS ROUTINE TIP #7:**
>
> Living life where you are, focusing forward rather than backward, takes time, practice and determination. The results you can expect can be compared to driving while looking through the windshield of your car instead of the rear-view mirror.

ROUTINE BUILDERS FROM CHAPTER SEVEN

1. Go back and read the four reactive mindsets we tend to form in our lifetimes, again. For each one, write out areas where this may have happened to you. Then write in a counter thought or affirmation you can use to reverse its affects in your life and/or career:

LIES WE BELIEVE ABOUT OURSELVES

_____

_____

_____

_____

_____

_____

WALLS WE BUILD AROUND OURSELVES

_____

_____

_____

_____

_____

_____

INNER VOWS

_____

_____

_____

_____

_____

_____

FEAR OF FAILURE

_____

_____

_____

_____

_____

_____

GREATNESS TIP 7: Realize that everyone has or will face adversity. You are not alone. The difference between being overcome by it and moving forward is to choose, every day, how you will process it.

GREATNESS TIP 8: Having a "Vision Statement" written is not enough. Constantly and consistently, we must keep it in front of us and utilize it in every area of life.

SECTION TWO – MASTERING HABITS AND CREATING A ROUTINE FOR SUCCESS

CHAPTER EIGHT – PLAYERS, ENERGY AND VAMPIRES

In the first section of this book, we dealt with multiple layers of heart, mind and physiological issues that prevent us from making progress in our Journey to Greatness through Routine. This next section is filled with ideas, tips and tricks to aid us on our journey. Before we dive in, it is important to remind you of two essential concepts:

CONCEPT ONE

As mentioned in the beginning, this process is a journey. That means that everything you apply must become a lifestyle. You must adopt a brand new way of seeing and thinking when you rise up, prepare for your day and deal with the tasks and challenges in front of you. This takes time, study, practice and effort. There is no "secret formula" to reaching Greatness. It is the small changes you make over time, progressively altering how you view your life and career, as well as, how you react to it. No one can read this book or any book just once and suddenly be transformed into the person they wish to become. We must commit to reading, rereading, applying and growing- consistently and unceasingly.

Now, if you understand and apply what you already read in the first seven chapters, you should be seeing yourself and the world around you, differently. The key is repeating what you learned and possessing an ongoing commitment to change.

CONCEPT TWO

It is absolutely, vital that you deal with your mind and your heart before any of these next chapters will have a significant effect on you. The "soil of your subconscious" cannot retain good seed sown nor can it produce a bountiful harvest if it is tainted with hurts, bitterness, hatred, offense and negativity. **Reading or studying self-help books or materials to improve your life or career will simply dissipate or quickly be forgotten because you have not altered your "inner-life" in order to receive these truths.**

As written in earlier chapters, the process of creating new neural pathways begins with the growth of new dendrites and neural pathways. Just like a newborn baby, these newly formed and growing neural networks need constant attention and nourishment. If they do not receive this, they can denature or turn into hot air after only 48 hours of neglect. How many times have you learned or read something that influenced you but ultimately did not change you? This is because you have not dealt with your mind and heart through the practice of creating new habits and routines.

I am reminded of an analogy/parable found in three of the synoptic gospels in the Christian Bible (Matthew, Mark and Luke) and the Arabic Life of Buddha. Aside from the suppositions of "religion", the wisdom in this story helps explain the significance of this important understanding. Its relevance is clearly universal despite its origin.

The first parable as written in the book of Matthew (the 1st of 4th Synoptic Gospels) in the 13th Chapter of the Christian Bible:

"A farmer went out to sow his seed. As he was scattering the seed, some fell along the path, and the birds came and ate it up. Some fell on rocky places, where it did not have much soil. It sprang up quickly, because the soil was shallow. But when the sun came up, the plants were scorched, and they withered because they had no root. Other seed fell among thorns, which grew up and choked the plants. Still other seed fell on good soil, where it produced a crop—a hundred, sixty or thirty times what was sown."

(Matthew 13:3-9)

The second is a quote from "The Arabic Life of Buddha" Bilauhar and Budasaf's version of the parable of the sower. In fact, it is almost identical to the one written above:

"The sower is the bearer of wisdom. The good seed is the good word. That which falls on the wayside and the birds steal is that which is only just heard, and then forgotten. That which falls on the rocky ground, which is wet and then dry when roots reach the rock, that's the listener who is good for a moment, when he hears it and his heart is ready, and it seizes his intelligence,

134

but he does not hold it in his memory, his intention or his reason. That which grows and gets to the point of giving fruit, but thorns make it perish, is that which the listener retains and understands, but when it comes time for action, which is the fruit, lusts stifle it and make it perish. Finally, that which falls on good ground and remains intact, grows, matures and prospers is that which the eye perceives, the ear retains, the heart preserves, and is put into practice with firm resolution, following the act of taming lusts and purifying the heart of defilement."[11]

Despite being deemed as religious in nature, this basic truth can be found in many other readings or philosophies. Interestingly, it describes the process of neuroplasticity in an accurate but parabolic way.

The birds and the rocky soil represents our hearts in a hardened state, when we are unable to grasp or hold on to new concepts due to hurts, deceptions and other blockages as discussed in previous chapters. The new growth of dendrites is simply not sustained as it is in good soil. Therefore, it can be squelched or simply convert into hot air within a couple of days.

---

[11] https://www.purplemotes.net/2013/09/01/parable-of-sower-arabic-life-buddha/

The description of the seeds sown in weedy, thorny soil reveals an analogy about what happens to newly formed neural pathways as a result of retraining or rewiring our brains. Despite the value we may find in new concepts, we reason within ourselves using the same old thinking patterns and thoughts of anxiety we always had. Just as in the choking of the plants, the cares of this world come in and consume our thoughts, depriving the new pathways of the necessary electricity needed to thrive and they simply denature.

Finally, the good soil, which retains the seeds and nourishes them daily, produces extended periods of consistent growth multiplying the plants, over and over. The same is true with creating new neural networks. In time, new growth carries the power to multiply our perceptions and can even change characteristics of our personality. Ultimately, we have altered our subconscious, thereby creating a new future.

The unfortunate truth to this is that the same process can happen to us in a positive or negative way.

THREE MAJOR PLAYERS IN ESTABLISHING GREATNESS

Greatness is more about WHO you are than WHAT you do. The three major players we will be discussing in the next chapters are crucial in developing a solid and powerful success routine.

ENERGY – FOCUS – TIME

ENERGY: If you have the energy to establish a success routine and desire to do so, but you do not have enough focus or you do not allocate time to work on what is required, you will end up looking like a squirrel on caffeine in the middle of the road. Looking in every direction but unsure of where to go and feeling pressured because you have not MADE the time to do what is necessary, first.

FOCUS: If you have the ability to FOCUS and work through your tasks undistracted, that is good. However, if you do not take initiative to motivate and energize yourself, you will grow weary and potentially lose interest. Furthermore, if you do not carefully plan out what you must do each day to create a well-managed success routine, time will always get away from you and you will become frustrated.

TIME: If you are excellent at planning and allocating time to do the things you know need to be done in priority order, you are bound to make some progress. However, without consistently generating the right energy while maintaining a laser-like focus, your efforts in time management will likely fall flat.

We must balance all three equally in order to triumph over our old habits, tendencies and patterns that have defeated us in the past. The remainder of this chapter and subsequent chapters are devoted to three components above. There are also plenty of tools, hacks and insights you can adopt in establishing the best routine for you.

ENERGY VAMPIRES

According to a study of 540 business leaders by Fast Company:[12]

- 82% were found not working at optimal energy levels

- 61% recognized they were working well below their best energy levels

- 21% stated that they were working above their best energy levels

"Energy reflects performance."

Theresa Wellbourne, eePulse, Inc.

EIGTH ASSIGNMENT – ENERGY QUIZ:

Take the brief energy quiz to find out how much you have. This quiz can also be downloaded and printed at:

http://greatnessthroughroutine.com

---

[12] https://www.fastcompany.com/3036840/what-your-energy-level-means-for-your-productivity

ENERGY QUIZ

Energy and Motivation are critical attributes to scoring high in Emotional Intelligence.

Take this simple quiz to discover how well you manage your own energy and in your influence of others.

Answer each honestly, based on your beliefs and behaviors before reading this book. Answer T or F (True/False), then, use the chart below to calculate your scores

1. ___On average, I need only 4-5 hours of sleep each night to function well.

2. ___I consume half of my body weight (lbs.) in ounces of water each day.

3. ___Fear is an effective way to motivate people.

4. ___Disorganization or clutter makes me mentally exhausted and less productive.

5. ___Everyone is motivated by the same thing.

6. ___Reading motivational books and listening to educational messages are a part of my daily routine.

7. ___People who are motivated are typically more extroverted by nature.

8. ___Encouraging others consistently only pampers them and is ineffective.

9. ___Laughter helps with problem solving and memory.

10. ___I spend at least 60 minutes per day "unplugged" from tasks or devices.

11. ___Eating healthy is great for the body but has little effect on the brain.

12. ___Nuts and berries are energy boosting and a regular part of my diet.

13. ___I believe in setting the bar unrealistically high for my team and myself.

14. ___I have learned how to say "NO" out of respect for myself and my priorities.

15. ___I exercise 3-5 times per week and notice a big difference when I don't.

16. ___Our world is so full of negativism, it's impossible to avoid.

17. ___Success means different things to different people.

18. ___Personal organization can help us gain and sustain motivation.

19. ___It is important to celebrate success for our teams and ourselves.

20. ___I maintain an excellent state of mind, which empowers me, personally and professionally.

SCORING YOUR QUIZ

Circle and calculate your total points based on the answers below. Add all together and refer to the scoring results.

KEY: 1=Incorrect, 2=Correct

#	Points	#	Points	#	Points	#	Points
1	T = 1 F = 2	6	T = 2 F = 1	11	T =1 F = 2	16	T = 1 F = 2
2	T = 2 F = 1	7	T = 1 F = 2	12	T = 2 F = 1	17	T = 2 F = 1
3	T = 1 F = 2	8	T = 1 F = 2	13	T = 1 F = 2	18	T = 2 F = 1
4	T = 2 F = 1	9	T = 2 F = 1	14	T = 2 F = 1	19	T = 2 F = 1
5	T = 1 F= 2	10	T = 2 F = 1	15	T = 2 F = 1	20	T = 1 F = 2

SCORE (TOTAL OF ALL ADDED) _____

TOTAL SCORE OF 36-40: You have a good understanding of what it takes to create self-motivation and energy daily. You are empowered and fully capable of taking on whatever challenges you may face with a positive outlook and a powerful resolve. Work on the areas you marked incorrectly to take your energy to the next level.

TOTAL SCORE OF 32-35: You are on the right track and have a fairly good handle on what it takes to energize or motivate yourself. However, it will be important for you to overcome the areas that scored a one on, if you desire to rise higher and accomplish more with an unstoppable resolve.

TOTAL SCORE OF 20-31: You are most likely finding life and career a struggle. In fact, it may seem as if you are constantly exhausted. The first step for you is realizing that motivation and energy are established, primarily by choice, lifestyle and practice. These attributes are learned. They are not inherited or thrust upon us due to circumstance. This is demonstrated by many historical "greats" who overcame insurmountable odds. Be sure to do all the assignments in this book to increase your score.

IDENTIFYING ENERGY VAMPIRES

Your next steps will include studying about what it takes to motivate you, inspire you and give you energy for each day. This means that you may need to give up some "energy vampires" and take on new habits for your daily routine (energy boosters). Changes in diet, activity, thoughts and mindsets are the only true and lasting solutions to this dilemma. If you desire more counsel or help, please feel free to visit, http://greatnessthroughroutine.

Energy Vampires are habits or actions that can drain your energy on a day to day. There are a few listed below to help you set up your new routine. As you read more about them, mark off the areas you would like to improve on.

Remember, it is the little things you do each day that can make the biggest difference in your journey.

___**#1 – LACK OF SLEEP:** There are conflicting reports about the average amount of sleep an adult must have to function optimally. Many reports say 8 hours, others say between 6-8 hours. The point is, if we neglect the amount of sleep needed for optimum function, it can severely affect our performance. In an article published in Scientific American, John Peever, Director of the Systems Neurobiology Lab at the University of Toronto and Brian J Murray, Director of the Sleep Laboratory, Sunnybrook Health Sciences Center agreed, **"Sleep serves to reenergize the body's cells, clear waste from the brain and support learning and memory. It even plays vital roles in regulating mood, appetite and libido."**[13]

Without adequate sleep cycles, we set ourselves up for brain fatigue, brain fog, anxiety, poor nutritional habits, illness and several other disorders affecting our ability to function at our optimum.

___**#2 – DEHYDRATION:** According to multiple reports and government sources, approximately 75% of Americans may suffer from Chronic Dehydration. Since dehydration is rarely recognized in most cases until it becomes severe, the majority of the population remains unconcerned and unresolved about it. Water is lost through normal daily bodily functions such as breathing, talking and urinating. It is also lost through sweat and bowel movements. Dehydration occurs when there is a lack of hydrating beverages taken in or too many non-hydrating beverages are consumed (i.e. caffeinated, alcoholic or drinks high in sodium/sugar)

You should be drinking no less than half your body weight in ounces of water, daily. Example: 128 lbs. in body weight would be 64oz of water per day.

---

[13] https://www.scientificamerican.com/article/what-happens-in-the-brain-during-sleep1/

When you are dehydrated, you will experience a reduction in blood volume and thickening of the blood, causing your heart to work harder and less efficiently. In addition, the circulation of oxygen and nutrients is minimized, reducing cell and chemical or hormone restoration. A few symptoms are headaches, fatigue, irritability, difficulty focusing, reduced metabolism and many other success-crippling issues.

___#3 – LACK OF EXERCISE: Below are some incredible statistics about exercise that you may not have heard in regards to your success. If you are already aware of these and applying them consistently, I applaud you:

- ✓ Exercising just 20-30 minutes, 3-5 times per week can cause the pituitary gland to flood your body with endorphins, significantly reducing the causes of depression while elevating moods. A few other benefits are increased immune system, expanded creativity, clarity of mind, improved learning potential and retention of information, along with many more benefits.

- ✓ Several reports, including one by Stanford University and the New York Times, have indicated that endorphins are 200 times more powerful than morphine. They can act as painkillers! Some even describe the effects of endorphins as a "euphoric" feeling or "runners high".

- ✓ Regular exercise also reduces cortisol in the body and brain, often producing better sleep patterns and aiding in weight loss. Some studies indicate as much as a 23% reduction in cortisol.

- ✓ Those who exercise regularly tend to have much higher energy levels and keener senses including the ability to focus on projects without becoming fatigued for long periods of time.

Are you convinced yet? There are many, many other benefits but almost no consequences for the average individual. Even those with disabilities can find ways to exercise within their limitations.

Exercise does not have to be complicated or even cost a lot. For example: Walking each day, taking the stairs, stretching, participating in floor exercises or even heavy lifting are all valuable and practical.

Note: All Exercise routines should be approached under the guidance of a physician, especially when health concerns or limitations exist.

___**#4 – LACK OF UPLUGGING & SOCIAL TIME:** Recent studies have reported that US Consumers spend approximately 4-5 hours per day on their cell phones. In fact, on average, cell phone users are checking their phones every 5-7 minutes. Often there is no real reason, just a habit. Added up over a lifetime, this calculates to approximately six years of time wasted on a device. Furthermore, if we add in television, the average in the West is approximately seven years. The sum of these two is 13 years! The facts are staggering and unacceptable.

Unless we are intentional, we will rarely get a break from the "blings and dings" of devices, day and night. We must ask ourselves what this might be doing to us and to the generations after us.

Some of the science behind device addictions has shown that the notifications produce a small amount of dopamine each time they alert us due to the reaction of someone liking our posts or sending us a private message. Dopamine even has the power to turn off certain receptor sites within the Amygdala (the emotional center of the brain), reducing cortisol and stress. Though the effects are small, these things can entice us or lure us into conversations that challenge us and possibly even enrage us. At the very least, they are stealing away precious time we could be spending in ways that are more constructive.

Obviously, we could list other distractions here but devices are one of the biggest, right now.

Some of the consequences of not unplugging are as follows:

- ✓ Risk of burnout

- ✓ Destruction of creativity

- ✓ Inhibitors of concentration and focus

- ✓ Resentment of our jobs or other obligations

- ✓ Unhealthy device addiction

- ✓ Potential "fall out" in relationships

- ✓ Reduction in productivity

- ✓ "Blue light" effects including insomnia

The addiction to devices has been on the rise over the past two decades. In 2017, Harvard Health Publishing released results of a "blue light" study in an article called "Blue Light has a Dark Side." The report found that when we spend too much time in front of blue lights (i.e. devices or LED lighting) or do so within 3 hours of bedtime, it disrupts our biological clock or circadian rhythm. This effect, suppresses the secretion of melatonin (the hormone responsible in assisting us to sleep). Additional studies reveal that it may be contributing to the causation of cancer, diabetes, heart disease and obesity. [14] These studies are still in the early stages but it is fair to argue that too much light exposure is having an effect on us.

I am not advocating that we destroy all of our devices or even ignore them as I have plenty of my own. However, they do serve a purpose, just as our dishwasher and other appliances do. It is a matter of learning how to take back control. It is placing priority on those things that will enrich our lives rather than possess our lives.

Unplugging also entails finding time for yourself. Time to be in the present, to reflect or meditate. Time to work on your goals and your dreams. Time to enjoy family and friends or just be.

___#5 – CHRONIC STRESS: Since we covered the effects of chronic stress in earlier chapters, I will not go back through the understanding of what elevated cortisol can do to your brain and your health. However, it is on this list because it is a major energy vampire. When we allow ourselves to remain in a state of stress or anxiety, it can wear us down faster than physical exertion.

We were not designed to be in constant stress and when we are, it destroys our ability to manage the three major players in establishing greatness.

---

[14] https://www.health.harvard.edu/staying-healthy/blue-light-has-a-dark-side

ENERGY becomes impossible to produce due to the physiology we are creating from poor thinking habits

FOCUS will rarely occur since elevated amounts of cortisol paralyze portions of our frontal cortex causing fatigue and brain blocks.

TIME management is seriously jeopardized due to the pressure we put ourselves under, ultimately creating a lifestyle of reactivity instead of proactivity.

Other energy vampires to consider are:

- [ ] **Disorganization or clutter**

- [ ] **Perfectionism**

- [ ] **Over-Thinking**

- [ ] **Negativity**

- [ ] **Trouble saying "No"**

- [ ] **Too much junk food or sugar**

- [ ] **Too much caffeine**

- [ ] **No clarity or written vision**

- [ ] **No written goals**

- [ ] **Fault-finding or Cynicism**

This is certainly not an exhaustive list but my hope is that you are beginning to pull all of these facts together and consider a routine that will empower you and help you to live a higher standard of life.

SUCCESS ROUTINE TIP #8:

Every thought, action or habit you choose to maintain is either pushing your forward or holding you back. Create a routine that will align your mind, heart and emotions with purpose and intention for a better future.

ROUTINE BUILDERS FROM CHAPTER EIGHT

1. Consider each of the energy vampires listed in this chapter and check off the areas where you have developed habits and patterns on a consistent basis.

2. Now consider how you will counter each one by including specific changes in your daily routine. Remember that you cannot achieve all changes overnight; you did not get there overnight. However, if you list them out below and develop a plan to work on 2-3 at a time, even 1 or 2 at time. You will make considerable progress and evolve into your greatness:

_____

_____

_____

_____

_____

_____

_____

_____

_____

_____

_____

_____

_____

CHAPTER NINE - INSANE FOCUS AND PRODUCTIVITY HACKS

As mentioned in the last chapter, the three most important skills for greatness are Energy, Focus and Time. Just as we covered the importance of creating a plan of action for filling our hearts and minds with the right thoughts and influences, we must develop a plan of action for how we manage our time and focus. Let's go over some practical focus habits and productivity hacks to improve the task management portion of your success routine.

#1 BRAIN DUMP AND PRIORITIZE

Nothing can drain you more than feeling overwhelmed by an overload of projects, obligations, tasks and deadlines. We can be inundated with so much to accomplish that it seems suffocating and sets us back from our intentions. I have encountered this myself and with many clients. The best solution is to develop a habit of taking five minutes to stop what we are doing and create two lists, one professional and one personal. Then "brain dump" everything that is on our minds into the lists, including every project and every area needing to be addressed that is plaguing you. You will discover an instant sense of relief knowing everything is in writing.

The next step is to prioritize each list. You can do so with numbers or highlighting in colors:

- ✓ PINK = Urgent

- ✓ YELLOW = Somewhat Urgent

- ✓ GREEN = Not Urgent

Stephen Covey writes about a 4-quadrant system in "7 Habits of Highly Effective People" which is also a phenomenal method of prioritizing our tasks, appropriately.

The key to all big projects is to "chunk" them down into increments of time rather than allowing them to overwhelm us.

Once you have both lists arranged, begin working out a plan of action to complete the top five priority tasks. Schedule reasonable time frames on your calendar, making sure that you are able to complete each item in the required time.

For non-priority tasks, break each one into a reasonable timeframe with deadlines for completion. For example, if you want to write a book, allocate the days of the week you can write and the time frames in which you will write. Keep in mind that you must be consistent and committed to staying on track or you will never complete them. Choose the perception that they are just as important as your priority tasks but with the understanding that they can be moved back on occasion, whenever needed. In all tasks, when we take time to actually schedule out the things we must accomplish, we increase the likelihood of seeing it happen.

Brain Dumping and Prioritizing is a critical habit to develop and maintain for life and should be done every week or at least every month. This will empower us to stay intentional and accomplish what we would otherwise, never finish.

NINTH ASSIGNMENT:

The next pages include a powerful 30-Day Goal Setting Planner you can use as a tool with guidelines and instructions. A download is available at http://greatnessthroughroutine.com. Take time to use it and create your first 30-day plan.

5 STEP PERFORMANCE GOAL SETTING (30-DAY PLANNER)

STEP 1 – List 10 things you want to achieve for your business/career/life in the next 30 days (print this page every month, re-examine and re-write your goals).

STEP 2 – Prioritize these goals in an order that will influence your life/career in the greatest measure. Use the second column provided to change the order of numbers, with accordance to priority.

1		
2		
3		
4		
5		
6		
7		
8		
9		
10		

STEP 3 – Begin with the Top 3 Goals and work your way through.

What RESOURCES will you need?	Who do you need to CONNECT with?
What EDUCATION will you have to pursue?	What OBSTACLES will you encounter?

STEP 4 – Break down the steps required by weekly, then daily task lists. **Print additional copies of this page to utilize EVERY WEEK.**

What must I work on this week to move forward in accomplishing my goals?

Step 5 – What TASKS must I complete each DAY to fulfill the work listed above and reach my listed goals?

MONDAY	
TUESDAY	
WEDNESDAY	
THURSDAY	
FRIDAY	
WEEKEND TASKS	

#2 PREP FOR THE WEEK AND THEN FOR THE DAY

The majority of the working population wastes 60-90 minutes in the beginning of each day trying to acclimate, prepare and figure out where to start with work projects. Often it ends up being emails, social media, chatting with co-workers and other time wasters. Then, at the close of the day or the week, we complain about our inability to keep up with projects and the demands of our jobs.

Ultimately, this kind of routine will only put more stress on us and deprive us of quality time spent at home due to the nagging feeling of not having accomplished enough in our workday. As a result, we can wind up in a downward spiral causing frustration, remorse, oppression, lack of peace and lack of sleep.

The remedy is quite simple:

While all is still fresh in our minds, take 15-20 minutes at the close of every week to write down all the projects or issues we must address on Monday morning, place them in priority order and set up any appointments or calls that must be made. Then take 5 minutes at the close of each day of the week (Monday - Thursday), writing a prioritized list for the beginning of the next day.

A great way to approach this habit is to go through emails and clear your desk. Often times, I find this practice is very effective in helping to create the list but also improves your workspace, dramatically.

Not only will we stay on task but also, we will close out our workday with far less stress and be able to unplug at home knowing we had a productive day and all has been put into writing for the next day/week.

#3 WEAPONS OF MASS DISTRACTION

The brain is not equipped to provide clear, creative focus when it is constantly distracted by people, notifications or other interruptions. Constant distractions can seriously infringe upon our creativity and our ability to accomplish projects requiring our full attention. In fact, when there are too many distractions, the consequences that result can produce multiple, even detrimental mistakes, compounding our frustration.

In Chapter Eight, we covered Energy Vampire #4 with studies showing the average individual checks their phone approximately every 5-7 minutes, even if there are no notifications. It has simply become a habit. In fact, they are now equating the dings and blings of notifications to be similar to that of a cocaine addiction. Here are a few more statistics on this topic as it relates to Focus and Time:

According to an article published on Adweek.com in 2017, statistics showed that we spend an average of 2 hours per day on social media platforms:[15]

- 40 minutes on YouTube

---

[15] http://www.adweek.com/digital/mediakix-time-spent-social-media-infographic/

- 35 minutes on Facebook

- 25 minutes on Snapchat

- 15 minutes on Instagram

- 1 minute on Twitter

If you add this up, it comes to an average lifetime total of 5 years and 4 months. Add in the addiction of television with the average lifetime total of 7 years and 8 months and **the final number of time lost is 13 years and 2 months**. These are years we could spend with those we love or investing in ourselves to become more.

Time is the most precious commodity we have and it is one commodity that cannot be bought back or renewed.

The solution is to become INTENTIONAL, every day by using the following tips:

- ✓ When you are working on projects, meeting with people, spending time with family or just unplugging, shut off all notifications and alerts on your devices. Choose set "check times" for looking at your emails, social media notifications, texts, voicemails, etc. Example: 10am, 12pm, 2pm, 5pm and 8pm.

- ✓ Devices are created to serve us; it should never be the other way around. The more intentional you become about scheduling times to check messages, the less likely you are to be distracted and "caught up" in BIG time wasters that are not propelling you into your destiny.

✓ Finally, whenever possible, schedule your biggest tasks earlier in the morning, even before work hours. This habit will give you a head start and avoid the day-to-day distractions that happen during highly active business hours.

#4 NEGATIVE ADDICTIONS

From the statistics, science and insights in the previous chapters, you should grasp the understanding of how critically important it is that we practice caution every day, in what we feed our minds and hearts.

All Addictions carry the same characteristics. Whether it's the blings and dings of social media notifications or addictions to drugs, alcohol, pornography, sugar, etc., they all produce a chemical reaction that creates a false sense of comfort or pleasure. Despite being short-lived and destructive to our livelihood, we constantly crave these "empty" pleasures.

Negative addictions are no different. When we listen to or participate in gossip, news programs or discussions that focus on the downfalls or tragedies of others, in a crazy, sick way it somehow makes us feel like we are better, smarter or more privileged. This thought process produces the same "feel good" chemical reaction in us as dopamine, oxytocin, serotonin or endorphins.

We can also become addicted to negative attention, which sometimes happens after we suffer some sort of tragedy or struggle. In the beginning, we appreciate the outpouring of love and attention, which is critical and life giving during these times in life. If not careful, we can become dependent on these responses leading us to subconsciously, create negative mindsets that crave more of this type of attention rather than working toward rising above it.

In all cases of negative addictions, we must ask ourselves some important questions and get very honest about our answers concerning negative addictions:

✓ Are they benefiting me?

✓ Is focusing on them the best use of my time?

✓ What affects are they having on me? On my family? On my future?

✓ Will remaining in them move me closer to my destiny or away from it?

✓ If I do not deal with them now, will I have regrets later in life?

SIX MORE GREAT FOCUS AND PRODUCTIVITY HACKS:

#5 TAKE WALK BREAKS EVERY 60-90 MINUTES

Stopping from a big project in intervals of 60-90 minutes can recharge you and refresh you. These breaks can trigger an onset of endorphins that will renew zeal, especially with projects that keep you seated too long. Even a 10-20 minute walk can increase brain activity, boost our immune system and increase cognitive function.

#6 EVALUATE LENGTH OF MEETINGS

One client approached me in frustration about attending so many long meetings. She could not keep up with her projects or complete her deskwork. We discovered that most of the 1-hour meetings she attended only required her insights for 5-10 minutes, at most. She was given permission to appear for allocated time slots and it immediately resolved her issue. (Who in the world said we needed to have 1-hour meetings anyways?)

#7 HOLD STANDING OR WALKING MEETINGS

Both types of meetings will keep attendees focused, interactive and on point. Not to mention, awake. Great thinkers like Steve Jobs, Harry Truman, Sigmund Freud, Aristotle and Charles Dickens swore by them. The additional benefits that result in these types of meetings have a multitude of benefits, such as better health, higher morale and increased creativity, to name just a few.

#8 SCHEDULE 30-MINUTE "THINK TIMES"

Often, we find ourselves so wrapped up in doing things the way we always have that we miss out on more efficient ways of doing them. They may be things we have done for years or even decades. Each week, schedule 10-30 minute "think times" to look at our lists and really think about each one, then ask the following questions:

☐ Is there a more efficient way of doing this?

☐ Can I recruit, hire or delegate it out and use my time more wisely?

☐ Is there a way I can do this better if I gain the right education or ask for experienced advice?

☐ Is this something else I really need to be giving my time and attention?

☐ Can I creatively alter this to make it faster, better or more economical? (i.e. think outside the box)

#9 THE TWO-MINUTE RULE

If any task will require only two minutes to complete, don't put it off until later. Often we will bypass emails, procrastinate on small jobs or neglect putting things in their place simply because we may view them as unimportant or unpleasant. Doing this only adds to our burden and lengthens our task list, unnecessarily. This, in turn, leads to more stress and creates a non-productive environment. Choosing to develop this one habit eliminates a vast portion of those "nagging" tasks that we so often delay in completing.

#10 ACCOUNTABILITY

Seek out a mentor, coach or accountability partner to share your goals with, who will hold you accountable and encourage you to accomplish them. This piece is highly valuable and well worth any time or monetary investment you might make. I often hear clients say, for the most part, they know what to do but just can't get themselves to do it. Even verbalizing what we want to accomplish to another human being can make us more committed than if we "go it alone." All of the greatest achievers will tell you that they did not reach greatness alone.

SUCCESS ROUTINE TIP #9:

Managing Energy, Focus & Time is more about managing YOU than it is about managing the obstacles we must overcome.

ROUTINE BUILDERS FROM CHAPTER NINE

1. Take a good look at all 10 tips offered in this chapter, again, and honestly assess the areas you need to work on. List them below along with specific solutions you will carry out in order to improve in all three areas:

ENERGY

_____

_____

_____

_____

_____

FOCUS

_____

_____

_____

_____

TIME

_____

_____

_____

_____

_____

CHAPTER TEN –
POWERFUL
PRINCIPLES OF
INFLUENCE AND
GREATNESS

The number one need of all mankind is so powerful that even newborn infants have been known to physically perish when deprived of it. Despite age, background, gender or position in life, everyone desires what I like to call, "Necessary Significance". From birth to death, we are all in pursuit of finding our place in society. We desire to be accepted, appreciated, valued and recognized for our contributions to the world.

As children, we run to our parents and proudly show them our attempts at gymnastics, coloring or art. Later in childhood and into our teens, we want to impress our peers by showing off, in both good and bad ways. However, the goal is always to same, we want others to recognize and appreciate us for what we can offer to the world. Even as adults, we strive for a better career, higher position, nicer house, car or anything that gives us a sense of achievement. Finally, in the winter of our lives, we cherish and seek after the relationships of loved ones, ever longing for their presence near us. We hold tightly to fond memories and live for visits, phone calls and cards or letters to remind us that we still matter.

In working with leaders and teams, I often emphasize these facts because it is the most powerful principle in creating a culture where people can thrive:

Teams develop strong loyalty when they know they are valued and what their expectations are. They want recognition for their gifts, talents and experience. They also want opportunities to contribute to the success of a business. When appreciated with a clear vision of their objectives, most teams will go well beyond expectations in performance.

This is also true in families, in communities and in all people groups. **Necessary Significance is the key to influence**. However, you cannot give to others what you do not have for yourself. If you are still struggling with unforgiveness (Chapter 6); or you have not worked on your heart and mind to develop a powerful, confident and compassionate inner dialogue (Chapters 1-4); or if you have not developed the right heart energy (Chapter 5), you will not be able to authentically practice the characteristics of influence.

13 CHARACTERISTICS OF INFLUENCE AND GREATNESS

The practices listed are simply that: *Practices.* You must work at them daily and expect each to take time to develop. As you continue to work on YOU, the rest will begin to fall into place. As stated before, there is no secret formula; you must be committed to consistent growth on this journey to GREATNESS.

#1 - HUMILITY

Some would say humility is thinking less of you and more of others. This statement is very general and translated two different ways:

The first and most common is that we put ourselves down or last, ultimately destroying our own potential through speech and inner dialogue but also in our daily habits. We may say things like:

- ✓ "I have always been sacrificial, putting others before myself, it's just the way I am."

171

✓ "I just can't, you don't understand my schedule. Someday I intend to work on my growth and fitness more. But right now, my family is more important."

✓ "You know me, a klutz and a procrastinator, lol! I have learned to live with it and I am fine."

✓ "It's just not my way of doing things. I am a very nice person but I have always been this way and I don't intend to change for anyone."

These statements are deceptive as they make us feel better about ourselves but they are a form of "false humility". They reflect someone who thinks they are doing their best but in their hearts, they know they are primarily looking for accolades or acceptance in their own shortcomings.

The second way of interpretation is less common because it requires more effort and more accountability. This form of humility is one of truth, authenticity, compassion and integrity.

People who exemplify true humility are never boastful. They think well of others but do not put themselves down in the process. They expect the best of themselves and never blame people or circumstances for things they are responsible for such as their growth, their mistakes and their shortcomings. They are not afraid to apologize when they hurt or offend someone but they don't "over-apologize", either.

True humility is demonstrated in a calm but strong state of mind that is fully aware and accountable to his/her behavior in every circumstance.

#2 - NOT EASILY OFFENDED

Imagine being invited to an elite event. You walk into a room filled with chandeliers and white linen tablecloths, glistening silver and china reflecting off the lights like diamonds in a clear stream. A sharply dressed man in a tuxedo, who seats you at a table filled with well-known and prestigious individuals, greets you. The purpose of the event is to recognize those who are influential and have done something to significantly impact society. Everyone at the table seems to be enjoying the dinner portion of the event including the performance. The energy of excitement laced with etiquette and courtesy fill the room. You are overwhelmed with a sense of privilege for where you are.

The program begins with the emcee clearing his throat and offering a brief introduction before the recipients of achievement are announced. One by one, the winners gracefully walk across the stage receiving their recognition with grace and humility. After about 30 minutes of awards, you notice one of the members at your table is seemingly anxious and the expressions on their face become a bit contorted. The awkwardness of energy combined with the restlessness they are displaying becomes obvious to the entire table. Several minutes later, the last award is presented and the room breaks out into applause with a standing ovation. However, it is difficult to wholeheartedly, rejoice with the excitement in that moment because the person who was clearly anxious has now become indignant and walks abruptly out of the room.

Soon after, a woman approaches the table and inquires of the whereabouts of this particular individual. Everyone at the table answers with uncertainty. She then turns and walks toward the doors leading out of the room. Within just moments, a loud voice is heard at the back of the room followed by shouting from others. Now, the energy of the room has completely shifted from a highly excited and positive experience to an unstable environment.

You look around and notice the room filled with mixed emotions, some chatting amongst themselves with concern while others remain focused on the winners and celebrating their accomplishments.

The emcee clears his throat, again, over the speakers and the crowd slowly settles down. Now there is one empty chair sitting at your table and it has become evident that the person, who once sat there, was offended.

You just witnessed how one person's offense affects an entire body of people who came to celebrate influence and recognize kindness in a hurting world.

Notice the distinct difference of energy in the room and think about when you have witnessed this scene before:

At the airport when a traveler harshly disputes his disagreement with the ticket counter attendee, affecting everyone around you, including staff, those in line and others observing.

A time your spouse offended you by a remark they made. A remark that you stewed on for an entire day, affecting you at work, as you seemed short and impatient with co-workers. Then you returned home still carrying that vile and negative mindset and affected everyone in your household.

No matter what we accomplish in our lives or our nominations, all of it is of no value if we allow offense to creep in and steal it away.

When reflecting on events of offense that occurred in your life, whether you were offended or the offender, remember how much you can influence others and affect our world for good or for evil.

Offense is not appealing to any one for any reason, even when the offense may be justified. Offenses are common and we all have to deal with them every day. Some offenses are from long past events and others are very fresh in our minds. If you desire to be influential and to have "magnetism", you must determine that when offense comes, you will choose to react in a way that makes others stand in amazement at your resilience and emotional intelligence. This does not mean that we will not need time to process hurts or scream into a pillow on occasion. It just means that those who are influential do not allow offenses to consume and control them.

Ask yourself this question: "Do I know anyone is constantly offended yet well thought of and highly successful?" Chances are, your answer is no.

"The problem is not the problem; the problem is your attitude about the problem."
– Captain Jack Sparrow, Pirates of the Caribbean

#3 - EMPOWERING AND THOUGHTFUL

A quote that I shared previously in this book, bears repeating again:

"People don't care how much you know until they know how much you care."

— Theodore Roosevelt

We truly build our future on how we perceive ourselves. Yet, how we perceive ourselves will always reflect how others see us. If your inner dialogue is primarily focused on how you can promote yourself or how you can help others recognize your significance, you create the reverse of what you desire. Some will see you as selfish and ill confident while others will see you as a "victim", always looking for someone to feel sorry for you or give you a "break." When you try to have relationships, you will struggle because, subconsciously, you are making them feel unimportant or insignificant because of your focus on YOU rather than them.

This perplexing anomaly is a vicious cycle for many. People who get caught in this trap often do so unknowingly and if asked, they truly do not intend to come across this way. In fact, just the opposite, they desperately want to be liked, valued and acknowledged. However, due to the wrong inner dialogue, they constantly struggle with how they feel about themselves and how others perceive them. This makes them only try harder to be recognized such as the teen that constantly gets into trouble. He does not wake up each day thinking about how he can cause trouble, rather how he can be important or noticed by his peers.

To be influential, make it a goal each day to look for opportunities to empower others and just be thoughtful. Below are a few tips:

- ✓ Remember their names and speak them when talking to them

- ✓ Recognize the accomplishments and/or feelings of others

- ✓ Pay attention to them, making them feel valued and significant

- ✓ Ask questions about them

- ✓ Look for opportunities to praise

- ✓ Listen without interrupting or forcing your agenda

"Successful people are always looking for opportunities to help others. Unsuccessful people are always asking, "What's in it for me?"

— *Brian Tracy*

#4 - CHEERFULNESS

Earlier in my career, I had the opportunity to build and lead teams. Every six months, I would conduct a team satisfaction survey. This would give me the opportunity to learn how I was doing and what kind of culture I was developing. I remember one specific time when I had received the results back. One of my support managers wrote, "You are very knowledgeable and compassionate as a leader. However, you could smile more. The people on the team, who don't know you as I do, often misconstrue your demeanor simply because you don't smile

177

enough." This really stuck with me and I made a genuine effort to smile more.

I am not saying that leaders or anyone has to smile all the time. However, when we do, we become approachable and we change the energy around us. I can think of several instances when a simple smile altered the environment and the mood of those in it. Furthermore, smiling is infectious and when we smile, often we encourage others to reciprocate.

It is also important to note that smiling releases dopamine, endorphins and serotonin that create a sense of happiness and can literally alter our moods, instantly.

#5 - SOCIALLY INTELLIGENT

It goes without saying that we must be socially intelligent to be influential. Obviously, we cannot expect to influence others if we struggle at getting along with them.

Socially intelligent people are those who show a genuine interest in others. They seem to have the ability to come across as sincere and thoughtful. The conversations of socially intelligent people always leave others feeling positive about themselves, about others and about the world in general.

A common characteristic of one who is socially intelligent is that they tend to be genuinely concerned about the affairs, thoughts, feelings and challenges others have. They are not interested from a standpoint of intrusion, judgement or pity but from the perspective of helping them to "rethink" their own perceptions. This is done through encouragement, kind words, listening, believing in them and never forcing their own ideals.

For example, a leader who is socially intelligent will not simply give out answers when things go wrong. They will approach each challenge with a resolve to raise the potential of his/her team by drawing out from them creative solutions and empowering them to overcome every adversity knowing that their leader believes in them.

"Leadership is not about titles, positions or flowcharts. It is about one life influencing another."

— *John C. Maxwell*

Another example is a socially intelligent business transaction. When working with a potential client, it involves listening to understand and staying open to new ways of strategizing. They will be able to reflect back client concerns clearly and effectively, assuring them they can see the issues from the same perception. Then, the suggested solutions offered will align with the client's needs because they have taken the time to listen, learn and adapt to the real issues of the client or organization.

In summary, Social Intelligence is approaching all conversations and challenges with the intent to leave people better off than how you found them.

"Most people do not listen with the intent to understand; they listen with the intent to reply."

— *Stephen R. Covey*

179

#6 - ENCOURAGING

In the beginning of this chapter, I mentioned "Necessary Significance", a vital need we all have no matter what our title, position or experiences in life. Encouraging others is one of the simplest forms of providing significance to others. We can completely alter how someone sees themselves and their future when we take time to tell someone, "Great job!" or "I am proud of you!" or "I know you can do this, I believe in you!"

Encouragement is not about flattery. It is about authentically recognizing the abilities, talents or contributions of others. True encouragement can vastly improve the perception they have about themselves and empower them to step out in areas they would otherwise never succeed in. It can also be used to reinforce behaviors we want repeated.

Consider the following relationships and visualize the outcome of each when you apply encouragement, consistently:

- ✓ Spouse or significant other

- ✓ Your children or other children in your life

- ✓ Family members/Relatives (especially those whom you may not currently get along with)

- ✓ Your supervisor or leader

- ✓ Your friends

- ✓ Coworkers

- ✓ Colleagues

✓ Strangers you meet every day

When you create a habit of encouraging others, you become unforgettable. When people think of who is valuable to them or who to invite to special occasions, job offers or great opportunities, they will think of you because of how you make them feel.

#7 - ACCEPTING AND EMPATHETIC

Having empathy toward others and respecting their differences is one of the most powerful ways to create influence in your life.

Just as we can push people away and create a poor cultural experience when we are offended, we will experience the same result when we judge others or do not accept them for whom they are created to be. Often, we are tempted to judge or criticize another when we don't understand their perceptions or that they are different than we are. In each case, we are always jumping to conclusions, assuming or thinking we know what is best for each individual.

I recall hearing about an incident that occurred at an airport, recently. A group of people assembled at the bottom of the escalator awaiting a tramcar to transport them to their flight gate. There was an older couple was amongst them, who were trying to speak to one another above the noise of the crowd. Out of the corner of their eyes, they noticed a very large woman coming down the escalator. Without realizing how loud their voices were, the old man turns to his wife and says, "Look at her, that's just awful! Why doesn't she do something about her weight?"

Most likely, the woman was already feeling very uncomfortable about being in public and she must have known others would talk about her. The man was speaking in a tone that was loud enough to carry, so others heard him and turned to look in her direction. Soon, the woman saw that the crowd she was approaching was staring at her. She was also close enough to hear what they were saying about her. As she passed through the crowd, it was evident that her eyes were red and welling up with tears. In this case, we can assume that the old couple meant no harm by their conversation, yet harm was caused.

Do we really know what that woman has been through in her life? Can we rightfully decide why she may have become the size she is? Do we understand the whole story behind her condition and furthermore, what was so important that she would have to muster the courage to travel on that day knowing she would be judged and ostracized for her weight? On a day when she needed acceptance and empathy the most, she received the opposite.

How often are we guilty of the very same thing? How often do we judge, condemn, assume and criticize others? Just as importantly, what has this approach done for us, for those judged and for our culture around us? Is it making the world a better place? Is it taking us to greatness or making us more influential? I think we all know the answers to these questions.

How about road rage? Do you become inflamed when others cut you off and then expect understanding when you accidentally cut someone else off in traffic? On the other hand, have you ever made an assumption about something that you had to apologize for later and then when the same is done to you, you hold a grudge against that person?

Accepting others differences without judgement is a trademark of someone influential. Others will feel safe around him or her. They can trust that their feelings, ideas or concerns will be respected and valued.

If they do not hear you judging and criticizing others in your conversations, they can feel confident knowing that you truly are a person of integrity and honor. In turn, this creates an admiration and respect that is rare and powerful. Having empathy toward others and respecting their differences is one of the most powerful ways to create influence in your life.

#8 - GRATITUDE

In Chapter five, we covered the power of heart energy and we walked you through all the emotions in terms of how they measured in magnetometers. Gratitude was one of the highest emotions measured and extremely powerful, emitting 500-600 magnetometers. In fact, it is psychologically impossible to feel a deep sense of gratitude and complain or be vindictive at the same time.

Gratitude has the power to heal the mind and heart of past hurts or tragedies in our lives. Those who, intentionally, choose to think about what they are grateful for every day, will find themselves feeling stronger, healthier and more well-adjusted lives.

Some might say, "Well if you knew my life and what has happened to me, you would agree that I have nothing to be grateful about."

When we choose to belief this, we are lying to ourselves or looking for excuses to stay bitter. We can be grateful for breath, strength, trees, flowers, the sun, the moon, loved ones, faith, values, beliefs, etc. There are so many other things that it would take many more chapters to list them all.

One of the assignments I give clients as a portion of their "brain training" is to come up with 9 things each week to be grateful for, write them down and think about them each day. This "Attitude of Gratitude" becomes a habit and alters your physiology (Chapters 3 and 4). The more you do to maintain a sense of gratitude, the more you will bring about a change in you that will become evident to all who are around you. Everyone wants to be around someone who is consistently grateful, just as everyone wants to get away from everyone who is consistently ungrateful.

I'd like to challenge you at this point:

Create a "gratitude list" and post it where you will see it (i.e. bathroom mirror or dressing area). Then speak it aloud with feelings of gratitude every day, first thing in the morning and again, before going to bed. Do this for one full week. If you are diligent, you will notice a difference, intrinsically and extrinsically.

#9 - AUTHENTICITY AND TRANSPARENCY

It is in our nature to believe that we can and should hide our flaws or shortcomings for fear that others may think less of us. This belief can have us wearing masks for every area of life. Essentially, "protecting" the real us inside so no one can get a glimpse of who we really are.

Living this way can create unnecessary stress because we have to work very hard at staying "undercover". It only increases our insecurities making life even more difficult. This kind of façade is exhausting and phony.

Although it may go against your former beliefs, I want to challenge you to think a bit higher on this one. The truth is that we tend to have a lot more trust and appreciation for those who own up to their shortcomings and gracefully accept that they are flawed, even laughing at themselves. The reality is that people can identify more with those who are less than perfect, than those who pretend to be.

Giving yourself permission to be you, sets you free! It also opens up new possibilities for expressing yourself, which can lead to better relationships, new job offers and many other amazing things.

Make it your goal to be the best version of you every day, ignore the critics and stop trying to be someone else. Just BE REAL!

"Have fun, be crazy, be weird. Go out and screw up! You're going to anyway, so you might as well enjoy the process."

— Tony Robbins

#10 - GENEROSITY

All of us have a desire to give back to something bigger than ourselves, to make an impact and to create a difference for others in our sphere of influence. However, those who are influential have developed a habit of looking for opportunities to give back.

When we build a reputation of generosity, people take notice. Whether it's giving to causes for children, veterans, physical disabilities or diseases, the rapport gained is undefinable in terms of cost or investment.

Some may reason that they would if they had the money to do so. However, being generous is not confined strictly to monetary giving. Below are some other ways you can develop a reputation as someone who is generous:

- ✓ Volunteer for a soup kitchen or other homeless cause

- ✓ Share insights freely through speaking pro bono at events, sitting on a panel or in one to one conversations

- ✓ Offer your expertise on a board

- ✓ Run or bike in a marathon to raise money for a cause

- ✓ Hold an event and promise a percentage of proceeds to a chosen cause

- ✓ Buy meals, toys or gifts during the holidays for the less fortunate

- ✓ Donate or help put together care packets for a cause

This list, truly, could go on and on but this gives you a few ideas to begin with. Giving of your time, insights, expertise or resources is never wasted and will always be a cornerstone characteristic of someone who is influential. **The world simply needs more people that are generous; make sure you are one of them.**

#11 - INTEGRITY

Integrity is one of the highest on the priority list of necessary characteristics. Even if you are able to represent all ten listed thus far but you do not have integrity, you immediately disqualify yourself as a person of influence.

The definition of integrity according to business dictionary.com is "the quality of being honest and having strong moral principles; moral uprightness."

Without integrity, you become untrustworthy; appear unstable and ultimately damage your rapport, even in the case of only one transaction or relational fallout where integrity is compromised.

Years ago, I assisted in hiring a manager for a team I was building, who seemed very authentic in the interview. They had a college degree, great experience and even the references checked out good. For months, they performed every task with precision and excellence. This person also seemed to connect very well with the team as well as leadership. However, they began asking a lot more questions about the history of the organization, about certain individuals and even about leadership. At first, it seemed innocent and inquisitive.

Then they started going out of their way to create a relationship with the executive leadership team, more specifically, the leader that was over their own supervisor. In time, this employee was able to use the information collected to manipulate their way into the supervisor's position and get them fired.

They held on to the new position for about six months but eventually, the web spun started to unravel, revealing many lies. Included in those were lies told in the initial interview when they were hired and their integrity was quickly, compromised. They were terminated, leaving a very poor reputation behind, along with a badly shaken team that needed extra care to rebuild and regain momentum.

Much like the story told near the beginning of this chapter about offense, one person could create a lot of damage in a brief amount of time for themselves and those around them. The difference between the story of offense and this story is that with offense, you can often redeem the damage done through an apology and a change in behavior.

However, with integrity, it is not that simple. Once you have created the reputation of someone who is not trustworthy or has selfish motives, turning it around can take many months or even years. In some cases, if the damage is too great, integrity is never really restored in the hearts and minds of those affected most.

"When you are able to maintain your own highest standard of integrity – regardless of what others may do – you are destined for greatness."

– Napoleon Hill

#12 - CONFIDENCE

Confidence is the stuff that greatness is made of. It is being willing to take risks; it is standing firm on what you believe in; it is not being afraid to become the person you were created to be. Confidence gives us the courage to step out beyond ourselves and pursue our dreams. To live in the moment and remain authentic in whom we truly are. It is dancing in the rain or singing in the middle of a crowd. When someone is confident, clear about their core values, and comfortable in their own skin, we desire to follow them.

It is a deception to believe that some are born with confidence and others are not. **All of us have the ability and the obligation to become confident in who we are.** All of us should make it a priority to work on our confidence levels, daily.

What is the Process?

As written throughout this book, the process is in our daily routine. It is formed in our thoughts, our hearts and seared upon our subconscious each day, from the moment we open our eyes to the time we close them at night. A few questions to ask yourself:

- ✓ What is my inner dialogue upon waking in the morning?

- ✓ How do I speak to and about myself, internally and externally, throughout the day?

- ✓ Do I offer myself the same grace and empathy that I do when others fail or make mistakes?

- ✓ Am I willing to step out of my "comfort zone" to meet new faces, take risks and just be who I am created to be?

- ✓ Do I spend time each day increasing my gifts, talents and knowledge to better myself?

We should be asking ourselves these questions and more, every day. If we fail to do so, we create a chasm in our "inner-person", an emptiness, a feeling of unworthiness, which is the root of ill confidence.

189

#13 - VISIONARY

It is not enough to share a vision with a colleague, an organization or even a community. You must have a vision for yourself. **Vision is the tie that binds together the accomplishments of today with the possibilities of tomorrow. It can be the hub of your universe, the compass of your journey and the climax of your destiny, all at once.**

A visionary is someone who lights the way and attracts others to walk with them into that light. It is someone who rejoices in hope and excitement the moment the sun arises and hits their face in the morning. People with vision walk taller and appear more resolved because they have an assurance of where they are headed and sense of purpose with every step. That sense empowers them with surges of strength and tenacity to accomplish things that others would deem impossible. In the Western world, people like Martin Luther King, Jr., Steve Jobs, Arnold Schwarzenegger, Oprah Winfrey, Eleanor Roosevelt, Thomas Edison, The Wright Brothers and so many more, were visionaries. They possessed an unstoppable mindset to pursue the dream in their hearts, against all odds. Despite failures, critics, lack of funding, credentials, shortcomings and hardships, they endured.

Whether you admire these individuals for who they are is of no consequence. No one can refute that they had and maintained a vision that materialized from nothing more than a decision to pursue their dreams. In fact, many of them started with no money and no influence, just the indomitable human spirit.

"Where there is no vision, the people perish."

– Prov. 29:18

All of the Characteristics of Greatness and Influence carry a distinct importance in your pursuit for greatness. As you determine what decisions to make in the road ahead, keep in mind that ultimately, we do not become what others say we are, we become who we say we are. If you are to reach the fullness of your potential, you will have to invest in YOU!

> **SUCCESS ROUTINE TIP #10:**
>
> There are two kinds of people in the world:
>
> 1. Those interested and have good intentions.
>
> 2. Those committed, at any cost.
>
> Are you INTERESTED or COMMITTED?

TENTH ASSIGNMENT:

Number a paper from 1-13 or write below. Then take time to really look at the 13 Characteristics and honestly assess where you are in each by rating yourself on a scale of 1-10. A rating of one means you are really struggling in this area and ten means you have formed solid habits and live out that characteristic consistently. Develop a plan for growth for any areas you rated yourself five or less.

1. _____ _____

2. _____ _____

3. _____ _____

4. _____ _____

5. _____ _____

6. _____ _____

7. _____ _____

8. _____ _____

9. _____ _____

10. _____ _____

11. _____ _____

12. _____ _____

13. _____ _____

CHAPTER ELEVEN – 11 TIPS AND TOOLS TO BUILD YOUR SUCCESS ROUTINE

The intention of this book is to help you understand that what you do every day of your life determines your destiny, personally and professionally. I would like to use these last two chapters to provide tangible "helps". They will assist you in creating a success routine that equips you in overcoming persistent behaviors and habits that pull you away from your destiny rather than push you towards it. As you read these, use the section at the end of this chapter to formulate your new success routine.

11 TIPS AND TOOLS:

1. GRATITUDE LIST

Write and re-write a gratitude list weekly to post and read, daily. Make this a life-long habit and be certain to use the emotion of gratitude when referring to it. Psychologically, you cannot be frustrated and grateful at the same time. This tool will empower you to maintain high heart energy and keep your focus on building the right neural pathways. Consider reading it every morning as soon as you wake up.

2. NOTE CARDS

Keeping the right thoughts and responding in ways that are excellent throughout the day can be very challenging. Purchase a stack of index cards to write out reminders, quotes, tips, victories or encouraging words of any kind to remind you as often as you need reminding. Brain training takes effort and each rogue thought must be "reigned in", immediately, in order to prevent regrowth of bad neural networks while promoting good ones.

Carry the cards like tools in a toolbox. Post them everywhere and anywhere you need to: bathroom mirror, computer, dashboard of your car, your wallet or purse, etc. In the beginning, it could be the "life-line" you need to support new ways of thinking but in time, you won't need them as much.

3. JOURNALING

For centuries, journaling has been an outstanding method of therapy that surpasses multiple other methods. It is a private place that can truly help us effectively, process and "dump out" frustrations, concerns, ideas, thoughts or events. In fact, it is a form of cognitive restructuring. When we write, it gives us an opportunity to reflect and reframe the words we have written, potentially, providing us with a new outlook. It can also be a place where new ideas spring forth and inspire, while serving a purpose to record these ideas for later use.

Finally, a journal is a fantastic way to watch our own growth and progress. Take time- weekly, monthly or quarterly to page back through and observe how many changes occur in your writings. Things that once upset you, no longer do. Ideas you once had, have come to fruition. Even prayers or thoughts you projected onto the pages have materialized, giving you new hope and zeal for what is possible.

4. MASTER LIST AND TASK LISTS

Nothing can inspire you more than a feeling of accomplishment and progress! Each year, create a "Master List" of everything you want to accomplish, both personally and professionally. Then prioritize it and keep it where you can refer to it, frequently. Each month or week, pull out one to three items and schedule time to work on them. For more detail on utilizing this list effectively, refer to Chapter Nine on Focus and Productivity Hacks. Download the Master List template at http://greatnessthroughroutine.com.

5. SPECIAL DAYS

All of us lead very busy lives and finding time to spend with family or friends can be challenging. When we are not intentional about setting aside time for them, it just keeps slipping away. Eventually, we realize we have not given the time needed to those we care for. This leads to unintended and unnecessary stress for us and in our relationships. Adopting a habit of "Special Days" can alleviate this in many of our relationships. For a significant other, choose one evening of the week for a "Date Night". It may seem trivial or difficult but remember that greatness comes from investments we make each day, whether in ourselves or in the important relationships in our lives. Keep it simple and live in the moment but commit to the date night. View it as you would a client appointment or a meeting with someone you admire.

However, don't stop there! Appoint a special day to each of your children, to your parents or any other relationship you value. On that day or evening, devote all of your attention to just them with no interruptions, play cards/games, go for walks, create projects or anything you both can appreciate. As each week comes and goes, those who are dear to you will know that they are valued, they are important and that you want to spend time with them. Your relationships will benefit as you sow these critical seeds and you will not feel as guilty. When busy days happen, you can remind yourself and your cherished ones that their day is coming up and you are truly looking forward to it. This will require some thought out scheduling and even, sacrificing but it is time you will never regret spending.

6. VISIONEERING TOOLS

Since we already covered the power of visualizing, there is no need to go back over it. Many of you may have heard of a "Vision Board". If you haven't, I would encourage you to seek out images on the internet so you can see what they look like. I want to suggest a couple of tools that are much easier to create and just as effective.

Vision Paper

Vision Boards can seem like a daunting and burdensome activity. Because of this, so often, they will end up an unfinished project. Even if they are completed, finding a good place for them where they will not lose their impact is another challenge. Sometimes it is best to simplify. Start with a blank Word document or 8.5 x 11 sheet of paper and place six images on it. Add comments or quotes under each one to describe what is in your heart. If you have a computer, you can just search for images to paste there. If you do not, you can draw pictures or paste on cutouts from a magazine. The project itself should take no more than 5-15 minutes to complete. You can duplicate or post these papers in multiple places, then change them as each picture comes into fruition.

Vision Cards

If you did the exercise in Chapter Two, you should have a well-written *Personal Vision Statement*. To keep it in front of you until you fully memorize it, put it on the "Note Cards" listed above. Alternatively, you can obtain some business card stock and put your vision statement on them. This way you can take these cards with you everywhere.

7. TRIGGERS

It can appear like there are just too many new things to remember when setting up a new routine. Our tendency is to fall back into old routine habits. However, we must change what is familiar. For instance, if we want to exercise and read more, perhaps we should break the habit of looking in the refrigerator or turning on the television when we arrive home each day. Triggers are a great way to aid you in creating desired new habits. The best way to create effective triggers is to remember the old adage by Henry Ford we mentioned before, "If you always do what you've always done, you will always get what you have always got." Therefore, your triggers must be something that is different from the norm. Below are the examples mentioned earlier and some ideas for each:

a. Exercise Daily – choose the same time of day to adopt this habit. Then attach the thought of exercising to another habit or event that occurs at that same time each day. For instance, if you choose to take a walk after work every day, you might attach the activity to removing your work shoes or walking through the entry of your home. If you have a pet, upon arriving home, when you see your pet, acquaint your mind to a walk. In time, it will become an unconscious habit.

b. Read Daily – You can apply the same trigger as listed above for exercise or you can set an alarm of some sort. You could just make it into an enjoyable event to help you prepare for the day, unwind or go to sleep at night. Curl up with your favorite beverage, in your favorite chair, and make it something you look forward to.

c. Stop looking in the Refrigerator – I had a client who stopped this and lost over 15 pounds. She simply wrote herself a kind note, on the refrigerator door, as a reminder to drink water or go for a walk instead.

Here is an example:

"Dear _____, Welcome Home! Grab a glass of water and go for a walk – you will thank me later!"

Triggers can be set up in a multitude of ways to create new habits. In time, the notes, alarms and choice points will no longer be necessary. You will be on autopilot, doing these things just as you do now with showering and brushing your teeth.

8. DAILY INSPIRATION

Once you finish this book, you might feel excited about creating your success routine and you may do an excellent job putting one together. However, as with all new things, we can lose our initial fervor. The idea is to stay inspired and motivated every day. I accomplish this and help clients accomplish this through morning inspiration, every day of the week. I have developed the habit of listening to something inspiring, educational or motivational as soon as I get up in the morning. Preferably, something related to my vision for the future. It could be an audio book, an online source or something pre-recorded. This way, I keep my thoughts intentional while my brain waves are still coming out of theta[16] and very open to suggestion. I then keep the audio running throughout my morning routine: Exercising, showering, making breakfast for the family, primping for the day, etc. On a typical day, by the time I finish my power hour and morning preparations, I will have listened to anywhere from an hour and a half to two hours of something inspiring. I even prefer to listen to something intentional in the car rather than the radio, while commuting during the day.

The BONUS to listening is that my family hears it, too. They have benefited greatly from it, even on days when not everyone was giving their full attention. Imagine playing intentional, inspiring messages in the background instead of the dreaded "news" or other distractions. Seeking daily inspiration through listening can change the atmosphere of your home and undoubtedly, the atmosphere of your heart and mind. If you remember Jen's story in Chapter One, this practice healed their marriage.

The second way to attain daily inspiration is reading books or articles. Choose materials that will increase your resolve for success and equip you to meet every challenge you face with the confidence necessary to rise above.

I attribute the habit of daily inspiration to be one of the most important pieces to the journey towards greatness through routine.

---

[16] Theta is a brain wave pattern that is between sleep and awake.

9. TECHNOLOGY

For those reading this book, who own devices such as cellular phones, tablets, computers and the like- there is really no excuse for not utilizing these devices to empower you, equip you and engage you in your success journey. Everything from apps you can download for exercising, meditating, scheduling and journaling to reminders you can set, along with websites you can visit for inspiration and information for daily growth. Devices can be a distraction or a gift. It all depends on how you choose to use them.

For those readers who do not possess nor desire to possess technology, think about creative ways in which you can utilize the "silent moments of the day" that will alter your state of mind. Try singing, speaking positive affirmations over yourself, reading aloud or just listening to the sounds of nature around you and taking it all in.

10. AFFIRMATIONS

In Chapter Three, we discussed forms of cognitive restructuring and there was a list of affirmations for you. This tool is a key piece to setting up a daily routine that will bring about the transformation required. However, if not done properly, they are simply "pointless repetitions". I use affirmations in the morning while I am on my recumbent bicycle. I have clients who keep them on their bathroom mirrors. Others like to speak out their affirmations in the car while driving. I am certainly not advocating reading while driving; just pointing out that a physical list need not be present for affirmations.

Whatever your method of using them, do it with authentic emotion, visualization and focus. This is the only way to produce the connection needed for there to be real change. Unless you can engage your heart, mind and soul, affirmations will not get the necessary electromagnetic energy to build new neural networks, alter your physiology, release neurotransmitters and change your heart energy. It is like turning on a lamp that is not plugged in and becoming discouraged because the lamp will not light up.

11.   RELEASE ENDORPHINS

The pituitary gland floods the body with endorphins in response to physical exercise and can remain in the bloodstream for up to 48 hours providing a multitude of benefits including:

✓ Reduced cortisol, the stress hormone

✓ Better sleep cycles

✓ Heightened immune system

✓ Prevention of anxiety and depression

✓ Reduced Pain and inflammation

✓ Increased pleasure centers, producing more serotonin and dopamine

Endorphins play a role in creating that feeling of euphoria often experienced by runners, known as "runner's high". Some studies found that the number of endorphins released could provide a powerful dose of pain relief.

As you build your success routine, do not leave physical activity out. Plan to exercise a minimum of 20-30 minutes per day, at least 3-5 days per week. If you can do more than this, the benefits will increase. **Daily, consistent activity is truly an infusion of power like no other.**

Try some of these methods of exercise:

- ✓ Recumbent Bicycling or Bicycling

- ✓ Walking or Running

- ✓ Treadmill walking (I do this an average of 5 miles per day at my desk while working)

- ✓ Yoga

- ✓ Aerobic

- ✓ Various Dance or Kickboxing classes

- ✓ Working out at the gym

- ✓ Lifting weights

The list is endless but you must discover a routine that works for you. To "fit it in", you must create a space for it. If you try to squeeze it here or there whenever it seems convenient or when you feel like it, you will never be consistent. Therefore, you will never experience the benefits from it. You might be the one who feels like you tried and it did not work for you. Only those who are dedicated enough to create a consistent measure of daily exercise will advocate for its advantages.

Consider getting a partner or making it a family activity. If that is not possible, think about how you can make it fun or productive. I will typically speak my affirmations while on my recumbent bicycle or listen to something with my earbuds that inspires or educates me during my floor exercises. Whatever you choose to do, it has to become a ritual or daily habit for it to stick. The time slot I chose meant waking up earlier in the morning, which has worked out fantastic for me (see Chapter Two for my morning success routine).

There are many more tools and habits. This list is just a start. I sincerely hope this will help you to get a firm grip on what it takes to create and maintain a new lifestyle of achievement, opportunity, growth and destiny shaping. Building a success routine is for those who do not want to remain in their comfort zone, coasting through life. Anyone from any stage of life or status can build one.

Below is a module you can use to formulate your success routine. You can also find this module online at:

http://greatnessthroughroutine.com

> **SUCCESS ROUTINE TIP #11:**
>
> Any project that takes sincere effort and focus to complete will always come together more efficiently and precisely when the right tools are used. The same is also true with your success routine. If the proper tools are not in place and used consistently, the odds of succeeding are vastly diminished.

ELEVENTH ASSIGNMENT –
BUILDING MY SUCCESS ROUTINE:

My Vision Statement is:

_____

_____

_____

My Specific Goals to work toward growing daily are:

1. _____

2. _____

3. _____

4. _____

5. _____

I will awake each day at:

_____

Immediately upon awakening, I will:

1. _____

2. _____

3. _____

4. _____

5. _____

While driving, I will listen to:

1. _____

2. _____

3. _____

4. _____

5. _____

I will learn to control my thoughts and attitudes throughout the day by using these tools:

1. _____

2. _____

3. _____

4. _____

5. _____

Upon arriving home, I will immediately:

1. _____

2. _____

3. _____

4. _____

5. _____

I will spend my evenings on things of value, which are vision aligned such as:

1. _____

2. _____

3. _____

4. _____

5. _____

Before retiring to bed, I will prime my subconscious toward right thinking in the following ways:

1. _____

2. _____

3. _____

4. _____

5. _____

Additional habits I will commit to work on adopting are:

1. _____

2. _____

3. _____

4. _____

5. _____

CHAPTER TWELVE –

APPLYING YOUR NEW ROUTINE AND ACTING UPON YOUR VISION

"Life does not happen TO us; life happens FOR us."

—Jim Carrey

INTENTIONALITY is the best word to use in describing the entire purpose of this book.

There are really two groups of people in this world:

GROUP #1

Those who live life as it comes to them, going day to day expending their energy and thoughts on the problems of the past or present. They typically "settle" into whatever hand life deals them. This group is frequently entrenched in debating about what is wrong in the world. It seems the only way they can rise above problems it is to pull others down.

This group traps themselves into limited vision under the weight of reactive thinking and acting. They live each day repeating the same routine, with the same perceptions, at the same level of knowledge, while keeping the same standards without fail, yet expect different results. When nothing ever changes, they grumble, find fault or simply degrade themselves for their limitations. They never really understand or comprehend why their ship does not come in.

The result of living in this group could be considered a victim's mentality. They are often broken, discouraged and feel as if the odds are against them. They typically maintain a survival mentality of "just getting by", denying there are any other possibilities and criticizing those who find a better way. They often judge and mock those who are willing to step up to see their dreams happen, because they are not willing to do what it takes.

GROUP #2

This group refuses to accept the "status quo". They are unwilling to simply, watch life "happen" to them. The individuals who sum up this group are only about 10% of the entire population, according to most statistics. Each day, they awake with zeal and energy for the opportunity of another day to work purposefully on seeing their dreams to fruition. They often arise in the early hours of the morning, long before sunrise, spending the first hour of the day empowering themselves by creating a strong mind and body.

Typically, this group has just as many problems as the first group but is unwilling to allow their problems to overtake them. Instead, they choose to use their problems as a springboard for growth becoming better, instead of bitter on life.

They have clear vision and purpose with a plan to carry it out no matter what it takes.

This group is relentless at taking 100% responsibility for where they are today and where they will be tomorrow. Whenever they encounter setbacks, critics, tragedies or failures, they bounce back quickly and search for answers, having little or no time to spend on negative influences or mindsets.

They spend each day with intentionality, making the most of every moment and utilizing that moment on things that push them forward into their destiny. They know their priorities and keep their commitments to the things that are important to them.

This group is one of the most misunderstood groups in society. Some people think of them as weird, zealous, over passionate, irritatingly positive or my personal favorite, "just lucky". Truth is the majority of them started with little or no advantages.

Which group do you wish to identify with? You are never too old or too young to make that choice and it is always **your** choice to make.

Below is a very brief list of those who started with absolutely nothing and faced seemingly, insurmountable odds. Yet, they all rose to the top, despite having minimal or no support:

- Jim Carrey – Actor/Comedian

- Dr. Seuss – Children's Book Writer

- Claude Monet - Artist

- Thomas Edison - Inventor

- Michael Jordan - Athlete

- Steven Spielberg – Writer/Director

- Les Brown – Motivational Speaker

- Sam Walton - Retailer

- The Beatles - Musicians

- Vincent VanGogh - Painter

- Charles Schultz – Cartoonist

- Elvis Presley – King of Rock and Roll

- Demi Moore – Actress

- Kevin Plank – Clothing Creator/Founder

- Soichiro Honda – Engineer/Founder

- Oprah Winfrey – Journalist/TV Talk Show Host/Actress/CEO

- Steven King – Author of Thrillers

- Steve Harvey – Comedian/Speaker

- Leonardo DiCaprio - Actor

- Emily Dickenson – Poet

- Thomas Jefferson – President

- John Paul DeJoria – Entrepreneur/Hair Care

- Billy Graham – World Renowned Evangelist

If you desire more inspiration, I encourage you to look up their stories. You will quickly realize how they are ordinary people just like you and I, who chose not to "settle". Against all odds, they tapped into their God-given talents, resolved to be intentional, worked very hard and found their way.

USING YOUR NEW SUCCESS ROUTINE TO ACHIEVE GREATNESS

If you have read and applied all that is in this book, you are now equipped to create a success routine. A new way of living that has the power to transform your future both personally and professionally. As long as you continue to apply it daily, the sky is the limit!

The benefits of keeping a daily success routine are endless, below are just a few:

- ✓ Stronger and healthier relationships, i.e. family, spouse, friends, etc.

- ✓ Greater resilience in times of tragedy or trial

- ✓ A powerful force in your current career, increasing your influence and setting you up for promotion

- ✓ A stronger state of mind and greater peace in your life

- ✓ New doors of opportunity opening, personally and professionally

- ✓ More energy, better physical health and clearer daily vision

- ✓ Greater confidence and a relentless mindset

- ✓ The potential springboard to an unexpected professional endeavor such as a new business or career.

I have had multiple clients start and succeed in new business endeavors! Most of them did not intend to do so before they began our coaching relationship. One example is a client who inherited an estate. The land in discussion had a lot of acreage and was in a perfect location to house a company. My client had a love and experience for the business they wanted to start, but for various reasons, the offer to obtain the property fell through. However, they did not give up. The spark was lit and their success routine was the gasoline that set them ablaze to find another way.

Long story short, they learned how to start the business they desired from home and followed through with the licensing to sell their own products. They now have their own brand along with multiple buyers and future plans to go into business full time. Their family is elated at the idea! By consistently, empowering their mind and heart, it opened the door to a new world outside of their "normal" day to day. Since writing this book, this client has kept to their success routine. They continue to see dreams come into fruition despite rerouting the map on their journey to success.

Contrariwise, I had a client who had progressed very quickly through our coaching relationship and was extremely excited during the building of their new routine. Not far into it, they birthed a concept for a business that had the potential to transform their life; a much needed idea, unique to their industry. They studied how to do it and worked hard to create the first prototype, getting better and better with each one. For not having much experience in this area before, the results were nothing short of amazing!

I was sure they would take it to the next level. However, soon after our coaching relationship ended, they allowed negativity to creep back in and stopped their success routine. Within weeks, they slipped back into the same old routines as before and their dreams faded quickly, along with their state of mind.

The lesson here is that whatever you gain from this book, from other books or even from a coach, if you do not choose to build and maintain new, lasting habits, you will end up right back where you started. For this client, chances are, all of the new neural networks they worked so hard to transform are diverting back to the old ones (See Chapters 2 and 3 for scientific explanation).

USING YOUR NEW SUCCESS ROUTINE TO ACHIEVE YOUR VISION

In Chapter Two, you were asked to write a vision statement and were provided with a vision mapping tool. Chapter Nine gave you many tools for planning, including "The 5 Step Performance Goal Setting Planner". Writing a vision statement does not always produce a new business endeavor. For some, succeeding at their current business or career is enough. However, having a vision statement and knowing exactly what you are called to do in order to bring that vision into reality are completely different thought processes.

As you contemplate the possibilities, you may be feeling excited yet somewhat uncertain. For some, discovering how to act upon strengths and talents with the right direction in mind can be a very challenging portion of their journey.

I have found that pursuing your greatness or calling is a process that begins with understanding what motivates you or makes you feel complete. If accomplishing your written vision is crystal clear to you, congratulations, you are one of very few! Just keep with your new success routine along with your focus and you are sure to see it to fruition. However, for most, seeing the vision to completion and knowing exactly how to get there can be quite vague.

In order to help you to gain some surety in the steps you must take to greatness, work on the next assignment.

TWELTH ASSIGNMENT:

Take time to write out 1-3 answers for each of the questions below to help you begin thinking about how to utilize your new success routine to accomplish your greatness and fulfill your vision:

1. If all obstacles were removed, i.e. money, position in life, obligations, etc., what would I really like to be or do?

2. In terms of a business or career, what do I love doing the most?

3. What positions, endeavors or responsibilities have made me feel the most fulfilled in my career?

4. When have I found myself the most committed, passionate and enthusiastic?

5. In what endeavors have I exemplified the greatest creativity?

6. Are there jobs or occasions when I felt the most confident and decisive?

7. What have others told me I am really good at?

8. Have I earned any special acknowledgements for a job, endeavor or project and felt like I could do it again?

9. Is there something I am good at, which I often take a strong stand on?

10. What problems do I see often and feel confident that I am equipped to resolve for others in the form of services, inventions or concepts?

11. What do I like to do in my spare time? Could it evolve into a career or be monetized?

12. What skills or talents do I have that come naturally to me?

13. Can I recollect any school subjects or projects where I excelled?

14. What is the one thing I am good at, that if I did not act upon it, in 5 or 10 years, I may regret it?

15. What traits do I have that could help me pin point the type of destiny I was called to: competitive, outgoing, popular, entertaining, social, creative, charismatic, etc.?

16. What core values do I possess which may play key roles in determining the best direction?

17. What volunteer activities have I participated in or wish to participate in that would indicate my passion and help me determine my destiny?

18. What careers or endeavors do I see my friends involved in that appeal to me?

19. Concerning subjects of interest as they relate to career or business, which articles or books am I most interested in learning more about?

20. Finally, what would be most satisfying to accomplish in my life or career: helping others, politics, teaching children,

motivating audiences, training leaders, bookkeeping, investing, starting a foundation, saving the earth, etc.

Once you have completed the above assignment, you should possess a fairly, good picture of where to begin your journey.

However, once you begin working on plans to move forward, realize that the line will not always be straight or predictable. While the original concept of your written vision may remain the same, the process and direction taken may change.

> **SUCCESS ROUTINE TIP #12:**
>
> No matter what you determine to do on your journey to greatness, the path that will get you there is, and always will be, mapped out in your daily routine.

In closing, remember that you will always reap what you sow and you are the only one who can alter your destiny. No person, circumstance or challenge can get in your way of your success unless you allow it.

I personally challenge you to put all inhibitions, excuses and fears aside. Be one of the 10% and choose to be relentless! Then, seek out and pursue your ***journey to greatness through daily routine.***

Below is a "Pledge" you can fill out and sign with an accountability partner, mentor or coach to ensure that you will not put this book down and forget the reason you picked it up. Go to http://greatnessthroughroutine.com and consider framing a copy:

ROUTINE TO GREATNESS PLEDGE

I _____ pledge to design a consistent daily routine for success that will take me from level to level into a new destiny. I understand that it is not the big things that create my future but the small things, done one day at a time with diligence, that transform. From this day forward, I commit to my new vision, new routine and new goals in order to become the person I was created to be in every area of life. By signing this pledge, I officially slate my course to Greatness.

Sign _____ Date _____

Mentor/Coach/Accountability Partner

Sign _____ Date _____

YOUR JOURNEY TO GREATNESS THROUGH ROUTINE COLLECTIVE RESOURCES

SUCCESS ROUTINE TIPS

SUCCESS ROUTINE TIP #1: Consider how you can rearrange your current routine. New habits are never developed by trying to "fit them in" with your old routine. There will never appear to be enough time. That is why we must create time for anything new.

SUCCESS ROUTINE TIP #2: When writing your vision, think about four strengths you possess that will get you to your ultimate destination in life or career. Under each strength write out four of each; goals you want to work on and resources that will aid you in the process. Taking inventory will give you a clearer picture of how much you really have going for you. It will also reveal capabilities or resources you forgot about or laid aside.

SUCCESS ROUTINE TIP #3: Just as your body needs healthy meals each day to maintain optimum performance, your mind requires the same. As you set up your new routine, try not to look at the changes as changes. Instead, view your new "mind diet" as a necessary discipline to achieving the end result. Your mind, just like your body, will underperform with a consistent diet of "junk food" such as TV, media, gossip, negative words, etc.

SUCCESS ROUTINE TIP #4: When we can feel and see the improvements and changes as we remain daily cognizant of our thinking habits, we can create consistent progress. This progress becomes evident very quickly and can produce a harvest, which inspires us to keep the weeds out and continue to sow the right seeds. The momentum we create in developing the right thinking habits is what will push us forward faster than we may expect.

SUCCESS ROUTINE TIP #5: Managing "Heart Energy" and achieving Cognitive Consonance is not a "once and done" process but a life-long commitment. It is a lifestyle. The only way to maintain the right heart energy is to be intentional about every moment of every day.

SUCCESS ROUTINE TIP #6: Taking revenge or holding a grudge is like pouring a glass of poison for the offender and drinking it yourself.

SUCCESS ROUTINE TIP #7: Living life where you are focusing forward rather than backward takes time, practice and determination. The results you can expect can be compared to driving while looking through the windshield of your car instead of the rear-view mirror.

SUCCESS ROUTINE TIP #8: Every thought, action or habit you choose to maintain is either pushing your forward or holding you back. Create a routine that will align your mind, heart and emotions with purpose and intention for a better future.

SUCCESS ROUTINE TIP #9: Managing Energy, Focus & Time is more about managing YOU than it is about managing the obstacles we must overcome.

SUCCESS ROUTINE TIP #10: There are two kinds of people in the world: 1. Those interested and have good intentions. 2. Those committed, at any cost. Are you INTERESTED or COMMITTED?

SUCCESS ROUTINE TIP #11: Any project, which takes sincere effort and focus to complete, will always come together more efficiently and precisely when the right tools are used. The same is also true with your success routine. If the proper tools are not in place and used consistently, the odds of succeeding are vastly diminished.

SUCCESS ROUTINE TIP #12: No matter what you determine to do on your journey to greatness, the path that will get you there is, and always will be, mapped out in your daily routine.

GREATNESS TIPS

GREATNESS TIP 1: To develop a new Success Routine, you must be open to altering your current schedule.

GREATNESS TIP 2: Managing your schedule to be more productive and fulfilling is the first step in reducing daily stress. As you design your lists, resolve to choose only tasks and activities that will give you a sense of daily purpose and progress.

GREATNESS TIP 3: Writing your personal Vision Statement will empower you with focus and clarity.

GREATNESS TIP 4: Managing your mind to focus on things that make you feel grateful or accomplished is the next step in reducing daily stress. As you design days into constructive thinking, resolve to choose only activities and entertainment that will push you forward into your destiny.

GREATNESS TIP 5: Ponder the mindsets you desire to change. Start thinking about tools that you can equip yourself with daily to begin setting your vision in motion.

GREATNESS TIP 6: Assignment #6 about forgiveness could be one of the hardest things you have ever done but the freedom you will have when you complete this portion of the journey will thrust you forward as if a dam has broken and the water that has been held back for so long is finally free to flow.

GREATNESS TIP 7: Realize that everyone has or will face adversity. You are not alone. The difference between being overcome by it and moving forward is to choose, every day, how you will process it.

GREATNESS TIP 8: Having a "Vision Statement" written is not enough. Constantly and consistently, we must keep it in front of us and utilize it in every area of life.

GLOSSARY OF TERMS

CHAPTER 1

Adrenaline (əˈdren(ə)lən) - a hormone secreted by the adrenal glands, especially in conditions of stress, increasing rates of blood circulation, breathing, and carbohydrate metabolism and preparing muscles for exertion – www.dictionary.com

Cortisol (ˈkôrtəˌsôl,-ˌsōl) - a glucocorticoid C21H30O5 produced by the adrenal cortex upon stimulation by ACTH that mediates various metabolic processes (such as gluconeogenesis), has anti-inflammatory and immunosuppressive properties, and whose levels in the blood may become elevated in response to physical or psychological stress – www.merriam-webster.com

CHAPTER 2

Neuroplasticity (nu̇r-ō-pla-ˈsti-sə-tē) - the capacity for continuous alteration of the neural pathways and synapses of the living brain and nervous system in response to experience or injury – www.merriam-webster.com

Synaptic Pruning - refers to the process by which extra neurons and synaptic connections are eliminated in order to increase the efficiency of neuronal transmissions. –

https://link.springer.com/referenceworkentry/10.1007%2F978-0-387-79061-9_2856

CHAPTER 3

Cognitive Restructuring - Cognitive restructuring is a core part of Cognitive Behavioral Therapy (CBT). CBT is one of the most effective psychological treatments for common problems like depression, anxiety disorders, and binge eating. These are some CBT techniques you can try at home to reduce problems with your mood, anxiety, and stress. – http://psychologytoday.com

Cognitive Behavioral Therapy - Cognitive-behavioral therapy (CBT) is a form of psychotherapy that treats problems and boosts happiness by modifying dysfunctional emotions, behaviors, and thoughts. Unlike traditional Freudian psychoanalysis, which probes childhood wounds to get at the root causes of conflict, CBT focuses on solutions, encouraging patients to challenge distorted cognitions and change destructive patterns of behavior. – http://psychologytoday.com

CHAPTER 7

Epigenetics - the study of changes in organisms caused by modification of gene expression rather than alteration of the genetic code itself. – http://dictionary.com

Quantum physics - (QM; also known as quantum physics, quantum theory, the wave mechanical model, or matrix mechanics), including quantum field theory, is a fundamental theory in physics which describes nature at the smallest scales of energy levels of atoms and subatomic particles. – http://wikipedia.com

CHAPTER 11

Theta – A brain wave pattern that is between sleep and awake.

RESOURCES AND DOWNLOADS

CHAPTER 1

Chart: Top 10 Stress Related Illnesses –
http://webmd.com

Chart: Symptoms of Chronic Stress –
http://womenshealthnetwork.com

CHAPTER 2

http://www.human-memory.net/brain_neurons.html

Dr. Caroline Leaf BOOK/MEDIA: "Switched on Brain" –
https://drleaf.com/media/switch-on-your-brain/

VISION MAPPING TOOL –
http://greatnessthroughroutine.com

CHAPTER 3

COGNITIVE RESTRUCTURING WORKSHEET –
http://greatnessthroughroutine.com

https://www.nejm.org/doi/full/10.1056/NEJMoa013259

AFFIRMATIONS CARDS (The Power of "I AM") –
http://greatnessthroughroutine.com

CHAPTER 5
https://www.sciencedirect.com/science/article/pii/S0022522396700946)

https://www.heartmath.org/articles-of-the-heart/science-of-the-heart/the-energetic-heart-is-unfolding/

CHAPTER 6
https://www.psychologytoday.com/blog/evolution-the-self/201501/don-t-let-your-anger-mature-bitterness

CHAPTER 7
https://www.uky.edu/~eushe2/Pajares/OnFailingG.html

https://yourstory.com/search?q=colonel+sanders

CHAPTER 8
Matthew 13.3-9 – NKJ Bible

https://www.purplemotes.net/2013/09/01/parable-of-sower-arabic-life-buddha/

https://www.fastcompany.com/3036840/what-your-energy-level-means-for-your-productivity

ENERGY QUIZ – http://greatnessthroughroutine.com

https://www.nytimes.com/1979/12/21/archives/chemical-found-in-the-brain-may-be-key-in-pain-control-derivation.html
http://med.stanford.edu/content/dam/Timeline/legacy-1979_goldstein_A33.pdf

https://techcrunch.com/2017/03/03/u-s-consumers-now-spend-5-hours-per-day-on-mobile-devices/

https://www.scientificamerican.com/article/what-happens-in-the-brain-during-sleep1/

CHAPTER 9
5 STEP PERFORMANCE GOAL SETTING (30 DAY PLANNER) –
http://greatnessthroughroutine.com

TIME SPENT ON SOCIAL MEDIA
http://www.adweek.com/digital/mediakix-time-spent-social-media-infographic/

CHAPTER 11
MASTER LIST TEMPLATE –
http://greatnessthroughroutine.com

SUCCESS ROUTINE TEMPLATE –
http://greatnessthroughroutine.com

CHAPTER 12
PLEDGE – http://greatnessthroughroutine.com

ABOUT THE AUTHOR

MICHELLE L. STEFFES, SPEAKER, CORPORATE TRAINER AND COACH

Michelle has empowered individuals and teams with her coaching methods for more than 20 years with her experience as a Leader, Director, Team Builder and Business Builder.

Steffes has completed over 10,000 hours of study in neuroscience, physiology and human behavior. She utilizes cognitive methods to accelerate growth, increase performance and transform self-defeating mindsets.

Michelle is the Founder and CEO of IPV Consulting, Founder of IPV Group Coaching and Creator of the 5 in 5 Performance Coaching Program and is featured in multiple magazine publications, radio programs and national media networks.

For more information, please visit: michellesteffes.com.